A Spell to Bless the Silence

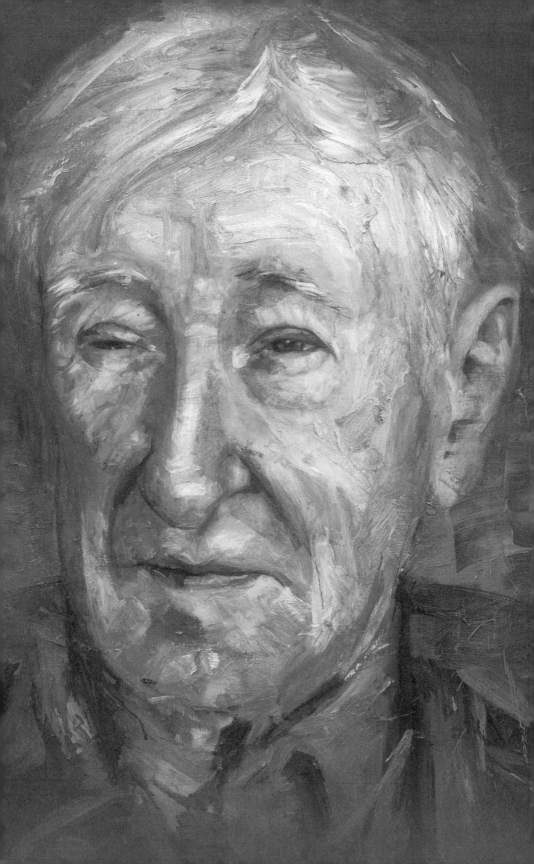

A Spell to Bless
SELECTED POEMS the Silence

JOHN MONTAGUE

WAKE FOREST UNIVERSITY PRESS

First edition

Wake Forest University Press
Post Office Box 7333
Winston-Salem, NC 27109
WFUPRESS.WFU.EDU
wfupress@wfu.edu

ISBN 978-1-930630-85-7
Library of Congress Control Number 2017963573

Designed and typeset in Trinité
by Nathan Moehlmann,
Goosepen Studio & Press

Publication of this book
was generously supported
by the Boyle Family Fund.

Contents

To harvest the "best" of a poet's work into a *Selected Poems* can be tricky. Should the poet him/herself make the choice? Or a relatively cool-eyed editor? John used to laugh, "I'm like the woman who lived in a shoe: I've so many poems, I don't know what to do."

Both John and I were struck by the fact that his more famous poems were not necessarily among his own favorites. "A Grafted Tongue" haunts the Irish imagination; "All Legendary Obstacles" stands with the world's greatest love poems; "The Trout" is at once homely and mystical. But John himself cherished a deep love for lesser-known lyrics: "The Fight" and "The Source," both sections from *The Rough Field*; the heart-breaking "A Flowering Absence"; and later poems such as "Paths" and "Silences."

The invitation to edit his own *Selected* gave John the opportunity to choose from his oeuvre not only those poems loved by the world, but those to which he felt a special attachment, either because a great force of emotion went into their making, or simply because he was pleased by them. We worked together, going through book after book, from *Forms of Exile* through *Smashing the Piano*, always reluctant to exclude a poem, as if the poor woman in the shoe had been asked to choose among her children. But at last, the selection was truly the poet's choice.

After the Penguin *Selected Poems* had appeared, John published three more collections of poetry. He had just finished choosing lyrics from those books for this Wake Forest *Selected* when he died. He found it hardest to select from his most recent volume, *Second Childhood*, because freshly written poems can feel closer to the heart, and so the poet's impulse is to include all of them. In the end, with the help of Jeff and Amanda at Wake Forest, I was able to compile a *Selected Poems* that encompasses all of John's published work. This is a precious book, both a representation of a great poet at his best, and a labor of love.

—Elizabeth Wassell
January 2018

from

POISONED LANDS
AND OTHER POEMS

(1961)

The Water Carrier

Twice daily I carried water from the spring,
Morning before leaving for school, and evening;
Balanced as a fulcrum between two buckets.

A bramble-rough path ran to the river
Where you stepped carefully across slime-topped stones,
With corners abraded as bleakly white as bones.

At the widening pool (for washing and cattle)
Minute fish flickered as you dipped,
Circling to fill, with rust-tinged water.

The second or enamel bucket was for spring water
Which, after racing through a rushy meadow,
Came bubbling in a broken drain-pipe,

Corroded wafer thin with rust.
It ran so pure and cold it fell
Like manacles of ice on the wrists.

You stood until the bucket brimmed,
Inhaling the musty smell of unpicked berries,
That heavy greenness fostered by water.

Recovering the scene, I had hoped to stylize it,
Like the portrait of an Egyptian water carrier:
But halt, entranced by slight but memoried life.

I sometimes come to take the water there,
Not as return or refuge, but some pure thing,
Some living source, half-imagined and half-real,

Pulses in the fictive water that I feel.

A Drink of Milk

In the girdered dark
of the byre cattle move;
warm engines hushed
to a siding groove

before the switch flicks
down for milking.
In concrete partitions
they rattle their chains

while the farmhand eases
rubber tentacles to tug
lightly but rhythmically
on their swollen dugs

and up the slim cylinders
of the milking machine
mounts an untouched
steadily pulsing stream.

Only the tabby steals
to dip its radar whiskers
with old-fashioned relish
in a chipped saucer

and before Seán lurches
to kick his boots off
in the night-silent kitchen
he draws a mug of froth

to settle on the sideboard
under the hoard of delph.
A pounding transistor shakes
the Virgin on her shelf

as he dreams towards bed.
A last glance at a magazine,
he puts the mug to his head,
grunts, and drains it clean.

Old Mythologies

And now, at last, all proud deeds done,
Mouths dust-stopped, dark they embrace,
Suitably disposed, as urns, underground.
Cattle munching soft spring grass —
Epicures of shamrock and the four-leaved clover —
Hear a whimper of ancient weapons
As a whole dormitory of heroes turn over,
Regretting their butchers' days.
This valley cradles their archaic madness
As once, on an impossibly epic morning,
It upheld their savage stride:
To bagpiped battle marching,
Wolfhounds, lean as models,
At their urgent heels.

Soliloquy on a Southern Strand

A priest, holidaying on the coast outside Sydney, thinks of his boyhood in Ireland.

When I was young it was much simpler;
I saw God standing on a local hill,
His eyes were gentle and soft birds
Sang in chorus to his voice until
My body trembled, ardent in submission.
The friar came to preach the yearly sermon
For Retreat and cried among the flaring candles:
'O children, children, if you but knew,
Each hair is counted, everything you do
Offends or sweetens His five wounds!'
A priest with a harsh and tuneless voice
Raising his brown-robed arms to cry:
'Like this candle-end the body gutters out to die!'
Calling us all to do penance and rejoice.

Hearing the preacher speak, I knew my mind
And wished to serve, leaving the friendly farm
For years of college. At first I found it strange
And feared the boys with smoother hands and voices:
I lay awake at night, longed for home.
I heard the town boys laughing in the dark
At things that made me burn with shame,
And where the votive candles whispered into wax
Hesitantly I spoke my treasured doubts,
Conquering all my passions in Your name.
I weathered years of sameness
Until I stood before the Cathedral altar,
A burly country boy but new-made priest;
My mother watched in happiness and peace.

The young people crowd the shore now,
Rushing from Sydney, like lemmings, to the sea.
Heat plays upon the glaring cluttered beach,
Casts as in a mould my beaten head and knees.
New cars come swooping in like birds
To churn and chop the dust. A wireless,
Stuck in the sand, crackles lovesick static
As girls are roughed and raced
With whirling beach-balls in the sun.
What here avails my separate cloth,
My sober self, whose meaning contradicts
The sensual drama they enact in play?
'Hot Lips, Hot Lips', the throaty singer sighs:
A young man preens aloft and dives.

Is this the proper ending for a man?
The Pacific waves crash in upon the beach,
Roll and rise and inward stretch upon the beach.
It is December now and warm,
And yet my blood is cold, my shoulders slack;
In slow submission I turn my body
Up to the sun, as on a rack,
Enduring comfort. In a dream
I hear the cuckoo dance his double notes
Among the harvest stooks like golden chessmen;
Each call an age, a continent between.
No martyrdom, no wonder, no patent loss:
Is it for this mild ending that I
Have carried, all this way, my cross?

California, 1956

FROM *Rhetorical Meditations in Time of Peace*

1. SPEECH FOR AN IDEAL IRISH ELECTION

Then the visionary lady
Walked like a magician's daughter
Across green acres of Ireland;
The broad bright sword
Of the politician's word
Summoned the applause in every square.

The unseen inhabited
A well, a corner of a field;
Houses assumed magic light
From patriots' memory;
Assemblies knelt in awe before
The supernatural in a shaking tree.

The light that never was
Enlarged profile, gun and phrase:
Green of the grass worn
On shoulder as catalytic token;
Acrid speech of rifle and gun
Easing neurosis into definite action.

The house subsides into stillness,
Buried bombs ignore the spade.
The evening light, suitably grave,
Challenges renewed activity.
The transfigured heroes assume
Grey proportions of statuary.

Now the extraordinary hour of calm
And day of limitation.
The soft grasses stir

Where unfinished dreams
Are buried with the Fianna
In that remote rock cave.

Who today asks for more —
Smoke of battle blown aside —
Than the struggle with casual
Graceless unheroic things,
The greater task of swimming
Against a slackening tide?

Wild Sports of the West

The landlord's coat is tulip red,
A beacon on the wine-dark moor;
He turns his well-bred foreign devil's face,
While his bailiff trots before.

His furious hooves drum fire from stone,
A beautiful sight when gone;
Contemplation holds the noble horseman
In his high mould of bone.

Not so beautiful the bandy bailiff,
Churlish servant of an alien will:
Behind the hedge a maddened peasant
Poises his shotgun for the kill.

Evening brings the huntsman home,
Blood of pheasants in a bag:
Beside a turf-rick the cackling peasant
Cleanses his ancient weapon with a rag.

The fox, evicted from the thicket,
Evades with grace the snuffling hounds:
But a transplanted bailiff, in a feudal paradise,
Patrols for God His private grounds.

Poisoned Lands *

'Four good dogs dead in one night
And a rooster, scaly legs in the air,
Beak in the dust, a terrible sight!'
Behind high weathered walls, his share
Of local lands, the owner skulks
Or leaves in dismal guttering gaps
A trail of broken branches, roots,
Bruised by his mournful rubber boots.

Neighbours sight him as a high hat
Dancing down hedges, a skeletal shape
Night-haloed with whistling bats,
Or silhouetted against cloudy skies,
Coat turned briskly to the nape,
Sou'westered in harsh surmise.

'Children dawdling home from Mass
Chased a bouncing ball and found,
Where he had stood, scorched tufts of grass,
Blighted leaves'— and here the sound
Of rodent gossip sank —'worse by far,
Dark radiance as though a star
Had disintegrated, a clinging stench
Gutting the substances of earth and air.'

At night, like baleful shadowed eyes,
His windows show the way to cars
Igniting the dark like fireflies.
Gusts of song and broken glass
Prelude wild triumphal feasts
Climaxed by sacrifice of beasts.

Privileged, I met him on an evening walk,
Inveigled him into casual weather-talk.
'I don't like country people,' he said, with a grin.
The winter sunlight halved his mottled chin
And, behind, a white notice seemed to swing and say:
'If you too licked grass, you'd be dead today.'

* In the Irish countryside one often sees crudely painted signs: THESE LANDS
ARE POISONED. This indicates that meat injected with poison has been laid
down to destroy predatory animals.

The Mummer Speaks

'God save our shadowed lands
Stalked by this night beast of the dead—
Turnip roundness of the skull,
Sockets smouldering in the head—
Will no St George or Patrick come,
Restore to us our once blessed
And blossoming, now barren, home?'

He paused on the threshold,
Clashed his sword of wood,
His swinging lantern on the snow
Threw blood-red circles where he stood;
Herded listeners gaped
Like goslings, as if they understood.

Bold as brass, a battering knight
Came roaring through the door,
Bussed the ladies on his right,
Smashed the devil to the floor.
Simple justice triumphs on the spot,
With straw, like guts, strewn everywhere:
False Satan struts no more.

A scene in farmhouse darkness,
Two wearing decades ago,
From which I best recall
Their faces like listening animals,
A storm lamp swinging to and fro,
And from those creaking rustic rhymes
That purging lament of bad times.

Irish Street Scene, with Lovers

A rainy quiet evening, with leaves that hang
Like squares of silk from dripping branches.
An avenue of laurel, and the guttering cry
Of a robin that balances a moment,
Starts and is gone
Upon some furtive errand of its own.

A quiet evening, with skies washed and grey;
A tiredness as though the day
Swayed towards sleep,
Except for the reserved statement
Of rain on the stone-grey pavement —
Dripping, they move through this marine light,

Seeming to swim more than walk,
Linked under the black arch of an umbrella

With its assembly of spokes like points of stars,
A globule of water slowly forming on each.
The world shrinks to the soaked, worn
Shield of cloth they parade beneath.

Woodtown Manor

for Morris Graves

1.

Here the delicate dance of silence,
The quick step of the robin,
The sudden skittering rush of the wren:
Minute essences move in and out of creation
Until the skin of soundlessness forms again.

Part order, part wilderness,
Water creates its cadenced illusion
Of glaucous, fluent growth;
Fins raised, as in a waking dream,
Bright fish probe their painted stream.

Imaginary animals harbour here:
The young fox coiled in its covert,
Bright-eyed and mean, the baby bird:
The heron, like a radiant italic,
Illuminating the gospel of the absurd.

And all the menagerie of the living marvellous:
Stone shape of toad,
Flicker of insect life,
Shift of wind-touched grass
As though a beneficent spirit stirred.

2.

Twin deities hover in Irish air
Reconciling poles of east and west;
The detached and sensual Indian God,
Franciscan dream of gentleness:
Gravity of Georgian manor
Approves, with classic stare,
Their dual disciplines of tenderness.

Tim

Not those slim-flanked fillies
slender-ankled as models
glimpsed across the rails
through sun-long afternoons
as with fluent fetlocks
they devoured the miles

Nor at some Spring Show
a concourse of Clydesdales
waiting, huge as mammoths,
as enormous hirsute dolls,
for an incongruous rose to
blossom behind their ears

Nor that legendary Pegasus
leaping towards heaven:
only those hold my affection
who, stolid as weights,
rested in the rushy
meadows of my childhood

Or rumbled down lanes,
lumbering before carts.
Tim, the first horse I rode,
seasick on his barrel
back; the first to lip
bread from my hand.

I saw the end of your road.
You stood, with gouged eyeball
while our farmhand swabbed
the hurt socket out with
water and Jeyes Fluid:
as warm an object of

loving memory as any
who have followed me
to this day, denying
rhetoric with your patience,
forcing me to drink
from the trough of reality.

from

A CHOSEN LIGHT

(1967)

FROM *All Legendary Obstacles*

In Dedication

My love, while we talked
They removed the roof. Then
They started on the walls,
Panes of glass uprooting
From timber, like teeth.
But you spoke calmly on,
Your example of courtesy
Compelling me to reply.
When we reached the last
Syllable, nearly accepting
Our positions, I saw that
The floorboards were gone:
It was clay we stood upon.

2. The Trout

for Barrie Cooke

Flat on the bank I parted
Rushes to ease my hands
In the water without a ripple
And tilt them slowly downstream
To where he lay, tendril-light,
In his fluid sensual dream.

Bodiless lord of creation,
I hung briefly above him
Savouring my own absence,
Senses expanding in the slow
Motion, the photographic calm
That grows before action.

As the curve of my hands
Swung under his body
He surged with visible pleasure.
I was so preternaturally close
I could count every stipple
But still cast no shadow, until

The two palms crossed in a cage
Under the lightly pulsing gills.
Then (entering my own enlarged
Shape, which rode on the water)
I gripped. To this day I can
Taste his terror on my hands.

3. COUNTRY MATTERS

    1.

They talk of rural innocence but most marriages
Here (or wherever the great middle-
Class morality does not prevail) are arranged
Post factum, products of a warm night,
A scuffle in a ditch, boredom spiced
By curiosity, by casual desire—
That ancient game...
                              Rarely
That ancient sweetness.

                              In school
Her hair was unstinted as harvest
Inundating her thin shoulderblades
Almost to her waist. As she ran
The boys called and raced after her
Across the schoolyard, repeating her name
Like something they meant. Until she stopped:

Then they dwindled away, in flight
From a silence.

                      But after dark
The farmhands came flocking to her door
Like vagrant starlings, to sit by the fireside
Pretending indifference, or hang around outside
Waiting for a chance to call her away
Down the slope, into darkness.

                                    Finally,
Of course, she gave in. Flattered,
Lacking shrewdness, lacking a language?

        2.

By the time she was fourteen she was known
As a 'good thing'. By the time she was sixteen
She had to go to England 'to get rid of it'.
By the time she was eighteen no one 'decent'
Or 'self-respecting' would touch her:
With her tangle of hair and nervously
Darkened eyes, she looked and spoke like
'A backstreets whure'.
                          Condemnation
Never lacks a language!

        3.

She married, eventually, some casual
Labourer from the same class as herself
For in the countryside even beauty
Cannot climb stairs. But my eye
Still follows an early vision when

Grace inhabited her slight form;
Though my hesitant need to praise
Has had to wait a sanction
Greater than sour morality's
To see the light of day:

                    For lack of courage
                    Often equals lack of a language
                    And the word of love is
                    Hardest to say.

5. ALL LEGENDARY OBSTACLES

All legendary obstacles lay between
Us, the long imaginary plain,
The monstrous ruck of mountains
And, swinging across the night,
Flooding the Sacramento, San Joaquin,
The hissing drift of winter rain.

All day I waited, shifting
Nervously from station to bar
As I saw another train sail
By, the San Francisco Chief or
Golden Gate, water dripping
From great flanged wheels.

At midnight you came, pale
Above the negro porter's lamp.
I was too blind with rain
And doubt to speak, but
Reached from the platform
Until our chilled hands met.

You had been travelling for days
With an old lady who marked

A neat circle on the glass
With her glove to watch us
Move into the wet darkness
Kissing, still unable to speak.

8. THAT ROOM

Side by side on the narrow bed
We lay, like chained giants,
Tasting each other's tears, in terror
Of the news which left little to hide
But our two faces that stared
To ritual masks, absurd and flayed.

Rarely in a lifetime comes such news
Shafting knowledge straight to the heart
Making shameless sorrow start —
Not childish tears, querulously vain —
But adult tears that hurt and harm,
Searing like acid to the bone.

Sound of hooves on the midnight road
Raised a romantic image to mind:
The Dean riding late to Marley?
But we must suffer the facts of self;
No one endures another's fate
And no one will ever know

What happened in that room
But when we came to leave
We scrubbed each other's tears,
Prepared the usual show. That day
Love's claims made chains of time and place
To bind us together more: equal in adversity.

10. A Charm

When you step near
I feel the dark hood
Descend, a shadow
Upon my mind.

One thing to do,
Describe a circle
Around, about me,
Over, against you:

The hood is still there
But my pupils burn
Through the harsh folds.
You may return

Only as I wish.
But how my talons
Ache for the knob
Of your wrist!

11. A Private Reason

As I walked out at Merval with my wife,
Both of us sad, for a private reason,
We found the perfect silence for it,
A beech leaf severed, like the last
Living thing in the world, to crease
The terraced snow, as we
Walked out by Merval.

And the long staged melancholy of *allées*,
Tree succeeding tree, each glazed trunk
Not a single heaven-invoking nakedness

But a clause, a cold commentary
Of branches, gathering to the stripped
Dignity of a sentence, as we
Walked out by Merval.

There is a sad formality in the Gallic dance,
Linking a clumsy calligraphy of footsteps
With imagined princes, absorbing sorrow
In a larger ritual, a lengthening avenue
Of perspectives, the ice-gripped pond
Our only Hall of Mirrors, as we
Walk back from Merval.

12. RETURN

From the bedroom you can see
straight to the fringe of the woods
with a cross-staved gate to re-
enter childhood's world:
                              the pines
wait, dripping.

            Crumbling black-
berries, seized from a rack
of rusty leaves, maroon tents
of mushroom, pillars uprooting
 with a dusty snap;

                  as the bucket
fills a bird strikes from the bushes
and the cleats of your rubber boot crush
a yellow snail's shell to a smear
on the grass
            (while the wind starts
the carrion smell of the dead fox

staked as warning).
                    Seeing your former
self saunter up the garden path
afterwards, would you flinch,
acknowledging
                    that sensuality,
that innocence?

A Bright Day

for John McGahern

At times I see it, present
    As a bright day, or a hill,
The only way of saying something
    Luminously as possible.

Not the accumulated richness
    Of an old historical language—
That musk-deep odour!
    But a slow exactness

Which recreates experience
    By ritualizing its details—
Pale web of curtain, width
    Of deal table, till all

Takes on a witch-bright glow
    And even the clock on the mantel
Moves its hands in a fierce delight
    Of so, and so, and so.

Witness

By the crumbling fire we talked
Animal-dazed by the heat
While the lawyer unhooked a lamp
From peat-blackened rafters
And climbed the circle of stairs.

Without, the cattle, heavy for milking,
Shuddered and breathed in the byre.
'It falls early these nights,' I said,
Lifting tongs to bruise a turf
And hide the sound of argument upstairs

From an old man, hands clenched
On rosary beads, and a hawthorn stick
For hammering the floor—
A nuisance in the working daytime,
But now, signing a parchment,

Suddenly important again, as long before.
Cannily aware of his final scene too,
With bald head swinging like a stone
In irresistible statement: 'It's rightly theirs.'
Or: 'They'll never see stick of mine.'

Down in the kitchen husband and wife
Watched white ash form on the hearth,
Nervously sharing my cigarettes,
While the child wailed in the pram
And a slow dark overcame fields and farm.

Hill Field

All that bone-bright winter's day
He completed my angle of sight
Patterning the hill field
With snaky furrows,
The tractor chimney smoking
Like his pipe, under the felt hat.

Ten years ago it was a team
With bulky harness and sucking step
That changed our hill:
Grasping the cold metal
The tremble of the earth
Seemed to flow into one's hands.

Still the dark birds shape
Away as he approaches
To sink with a hovering
Fury of open beaks —
Starling, magpie, crow ride
A gunmetal sheen of gaping earth.

Clear the Way

Jimmy Drummond used bad language at school,
All the four-letter words, like a drip from a drain.
At six he knew how little children were born,
As well he might, since his mother bore nine,
Six after her soldier husband left for the wars

Under the motto of the Royal Irish, *Clear the Way!*
When his body returned from England

The authorities told them not to unscrew the lid
To see the remnants of Fusilier Drummond inside —
A chancey hand grenade had left nothing to hide

And Jimmy's mother was pregnant at the graveside —
Clear the way, and nothing to hide.
Love came to her punctually each springtime,
Settled in the ditch under some labouring man:
'It comes over you, you have to lie down.'

Her only revenge on her hasty lovers
Was to call each child after its father,
Which the locals admired, and seeing her saunter
To collect the pension of her soldier husband
Trailed by her army of baby Irregulars:

Some of whom made soldiers for foreign wars,
Some supplied factories in England.
Jimmy Drummond was the eldest but died younger than any
When he fell from a scaffolding in Coventry
Condemned, like all his family, to *Clear the Way!*

Forge

The whole shed smelt of dead iron:
the dented teeth of a harrow,
the feminine pathos of donkeys' shoes.

A labourer backed in a Clydesdale.
Hugely fretful, its nostrils dilated
while the smith viced a hoof

in his apron, wrestling it
to calmness, as he sheared the pith
like wood-chips, to a rough circle.

Then the bellows sang in the tall chimney
waking the sleeping metal, to leap
on the anvil. As I was slowly

beaten to a matching curve
the walls echoed the stress
of the verb *to forge*.

Time Out

The donkey sat down on the roadside
Suddenly, as though tired of carrying
His cross. There was a varnish
Of sweat on his coat, and a fly
On his left ear. The tinker
Beating him finally gave in,
Sat on the grass himself, prying
His coat for his pipe. The donkey
(Not beautiful but more fragile
Than any swan, with his small
Front hooves folded under him)
Gathered enough courage to raise
That fearsome head, lipping a daisy,
As if to say — slowly, contentedly —
Yes, there is a virtue in movement,
But only going so far, so fast,
Sucking the sweet grass of stubbornness.

FROM *A Chosen Light*

1. 11 RUE DAGUERRE

At night, sometimes, when I cannot sleep
I go to the *atelier* door
And smell the earth of the garden.

It exhales softly,
Especially now, approaching springtime,
When tendrils of green are plaited

Across the humus, desperately frail
In their passage against
The dark, unredeemed parcels of earth.

There is white light on the cobblestones
And in the apartment house opposite —
All four floors — silence.

In that stillness — soft but luminously exact,
A chosen light — I notice that
The tips of the lately grafted cherry tree

Are a firm and lacquered black.

2. SALUTE, IN PASSING, FOR SAM

The voyagers we cannot follow
Are the most haunting. That face
Time has worn to a fastidious mask
Chides me, as one strict master

Strides through the Luxembourg.
Surrounded by children, lovers,
His thoughts are rigorous as trees
Reduced by winter. While the water
Parts for tiny white-rigged yachts
He plots an icy human mathematics —
Proving what content sighs when all
Is lost, what wit flares from nothingness:
His handsome hawk head is sacrificial
As he weathers to how man now is.

The Broken Shape

I. ENCLOSURE

Through the poplars we spy the broken
Shape of the château. No one wishes
To visit now, although sections
Of family stay through the summer,
Children chasing, gathering serrated
Pine cones. Around the landscaped woods
The high stone wall no longer defines
But falters.

       As at twilight
Under the portraits of the long
Gallery (the ambassador to Russia,
The high-booted elegance of Turenne's
Aide-de-camp) the adults assemble
To the light ritual of a conversation
Determined before they were born.
Close to Le Figaro on the inlaid
Table rests l'Almanach du Gotha,

A closed book for a closed and
Closing world.

           Though the window
Still frames the steeple, frail
As a lady's finger, of the family
Church where they were baptized
And married, with the school built
By their father for the peasants' good,
And the Mayor's house where, till lately,
He was master. A pattern of use
Dwindles to aesthetic views

                 Except
In this last room where blue Sèvres,
A bare-breasted Maenad, and dull
Gold of panelled walls preserve
The restraints of a style, over which
The massive teardrops of the chandelier
Suspend, shifting soundlessly,
Like a mobile.

2. THE CENTENARIAN

All afternoon we assemble, a cluster
of children, grandchildren, great-
grandchildren, in-laws like myself
come to celebrate this scant-haired
talkative old lady's
long delaying action against death.

While technicians scurry to arrange
cables, and test for sound,
calmly on the lawn we dispose

ourselves; spokes of a wheel
radiating from that strict centre
where she holds her ground.

Skullcap like a Rembrandt Jew,
jowls weathered past yellow to old gold,
the hands in her lap discreetly folded
shelter a black morocco purse
containing (so the awed family claim)
a sound portfolio from the Paris *bourse*.

As the cameras whir she recites
her life, with the frightening babble
of the age liberated, entirely free:
how she knew the young Hussar captain
loved her, as passing her window
every morning he lifted his *képi*:

how she drove through French and enemy lines
to recover her handsome cavalier son
buried in No Man's Land;
but the hasty planks of her home-
made coffin were too short:
his boot came away in her hand.

She does not raise her failing eyes
to heaven, to attest what she has undergone,
but treats Him like a gentleman
who will know how things are done
when she is finally gathered upwards
with, but not like, everyone...

The Split Lyre

after Zadkine

On the frost-held
field Orpheus
strides, his greaves
bleak with light,
the split lyre
silver hard
in his hands;
sleek after him
the damp-tongued
cringing hounds.

An unaccountable
desire to kneel,
to pray, pulls
my hands but
his head is not
a crown of thorns:
a great antlered
stag, pity
shrinks from
those horns.

Beyond the Liss*

for Robert Duncan

Seán the hunchback, sadly
Walking the road at evening
Hears an errant music,
Clear, strange, beautiful,

And thrusts his moon face
Over the wet hedge
To spy a ring of noble
Figures dancing, with —

A rose at the centre —
The lustrous princess.

Humbly he pleads to join,
Saying, 'Pardon my ugliness,
Reward my patience,
Heavenly governess.'

Presto! Like the frog prince
His hump grows feather-
Light, his back splits,
And he steps forth, shining

Into the world of ideal
Movement where (stripped
Of stale selfishness,
Curdled envy) all

Act not as they are
But might wish to be —
Planets assumed in
A sidereal harmony —

Strawfoot Seán
Limber as any.

But slowly old habits
Reassert themselves, he
Quarrels with pure gift,
Declares the boredom

Of a perfect music
And, with goatish nastiness,
Seeks first to insult,
Then rape, the elegant princess.

Presto! With a sound
Like a rusty tearing
He finds himself lifted
Again through the air

To land, sprawling,
Outside the hedge,
His satchel hump securely
Back on his back.

*Seán the hunchback, sadly
Walking the road at evening...*

* Liss (lios): Irish for a fairy mound, or ring-fort.

from

TIDES

(1970)

Summer Storm

1. A Door Banging

Downstairs, a door
banging, like a
blow upon sleep,

pain bleeding
away in gouts
of accusation &

counter accusation:
heart's release
of bitter speech.

2. Mosquito Hunt

Heat contracts the
walls, smeared with
the bodies of insects

we crush, absurd-
ly balanced on the
springs of the bed

twin shadows on
the wall rising
& falling as

we swoop &
quarrel, like
wide-winged bats.

3. TIDES

The window blown
open that summer
night, a full moon

occupying the sky
with a pressure of
underwater light,

a chill radiance
glossing the titles
behind your head

& the rectangle
of the bed where,
after long separation,

we begin to make
love quietly, bodies
turning like fish

in obedience to
the pull & tug
of your great tides.

Coming Events

In the Groeningemuseum at Bruges there is a picture by Gerard
David of a man being flayed. Four craftsmen are concerned with the
figure on the table: one is opening the left arm, another lifting away
the right nipple, a third incising the right arm while the last (his
knife caught between his teeth) is unwinding the results of his la-
bour so as to display the rich network of veins under the skin of the

left leg. The only expression in the faces of those looking on is a mild admiration: the burgomaster has caught up the white folds of his ermine gown and is gazing into the middle distance. It is difficult even to say that there is any expression on the face of the victim, although his teeth are gritted and the cords attaching his wrists to the legs of the table are stretched tight. The whole scene may be intended as an allegory of human suffering but what the line of perspective leads us to admire is the brown calfskin of the principal executioner's boots.

Special Delivery

The spider's web
of your handwriting
on a blue envelope

brings up too much
to bear, old seasick-
ness of love, retch

of sentiment, night
& day devoured by
the worm of delight

which turns to
feed upon itself;
emotion running so

wildly to seed
between us that
it assumes a third,

a ghostly or child's
face, the soft skull
frail as an eggshell

& the life-cord
of the emerging body —
fish, reptile, bird —

which trails
like the cable
of an astronaut

as we whirl & turn
in our bubble of
blood & sperm

before the gravities
of earth claim us
from limitless space.

*

Now, light years later,
your nostalgic letter
admitting failure,

claiming forgiveness.
When fire pales to
so faint an ash,

so frail a design,
why measure guilt,
your fault or mine:

but blood seeps where
I sign before tearing
down the perforated line.

Life Class

The infinite softness
& complexity of a body
in repose. The hinge

of the ankle bone de-
fines the flat space
of a foot, its puckered

flesh & almost arch.
The calf's heavy curve
sweeping down against

the bony shin, or up
to the warm bulges and
hollows of the knee

describes a line of
gravity, energy as
from shoulder knob

to knuckle, the arm
cascades, round the
elbow, over the wrist.

The whole body a system
of checks & balances —
those natural shapes

a sculptor celebrates,
sea-worn caves, pools,
boulders, tree trunks —

or, at every hand's turn,
a crop of temptation:
arm & thigh opening

on softer, more secret
areas, hair sprouting
crevices, odorous nooks

& crannies of love,
awaiting the impress
of desire, a fervent

homage, or tempting
to an extinction of
burrowing blindness.

(Deviously uncurling
from the hot clothes
of shame, a desert

father's dream of
sluttish nakedness,
demon with inflamed

breasts, dangling
tresses to drag man
down to hell's gaping

vaginal mouth.)

> To see the model
> as simply human

a mild housewife
earning pocket money
for husband, child,

is to feel the dark
centuries peel away
to the innocence of

the white track on
her shoulders where
above brown flesh

the brassiere lifts
to show the quiet of
unsunned breasts &

to mourn & cherish
each melancholy proof
of mortality's grudge

against perfection:
the appendix scar
lacing the stomach

the pale stitches on
the wailing wall of
the rib-cage where

the heart obediently
pumps.

What homage
is worthy for such

a gentle unveiling?
To nibble her ten
toes, in an ecstasy

of love, to drink
hair, like water?
(Fashion designers

would flatten her
breasts, level the
curves of arse &

stomach, moulding
the mother lode
that pulses beneath

to a uniformity
of robot bliss.)

On cartridge paper

an army of pencils
deploy silently to
lure her into their

net of lines while
from & above her
chilled, cramped

body blossoms
a late flower:
her tired smile.

To Cease

for Samuel Beckett

To cease
to be human.

To be
a rock down
which rain pours,
a granite jaw
slowly discoloured.

Or a statue
sporting a giant's beard
of verdigris or rust
in some forgotten
village square.

A tree worn
by the prevailing winds
to a diagram of
tangled branches:
gnarled, sapless, alone.

To cease
to be human
and let birds soil
your skull, animals rest
in the crook of your arm.

To become
an object, honoured
or not, as the occasion demands,
while time bends you slowly
back to the ground.

FROM *Sea Changes*

4. WINE DARK SEA

For there is no sea
it is all a dream
there is no sea
except in the tangle
of our minds:
the wine dark
sea of history
on which we all turn
turn and thresh
       and disappear.

from

THE ROUGH FIELD

(1972)

1.

Catching a bus at Victoria Station,
Symbol of Belfast in its iron bleakness,
We ride through narrow huckster streets
(Small lamps bright before the Sacred Heart,
Bunting tagged for some religious feast)
To where Cavehill and Divis, stern presences,
Brood over a wilderness of cinemas and shops,
Victorian red-brick villas, framed with aerials,
Bushmills hoardings, Orange and Legion Halls.
A fringe of trees affords some ease at last
From all this dour, despoiled inheritance,
The shabby throughotherness of outskirts:
'God is Love', chalked on a grimy wall
Mocks a culture where constraint is all.

Through half of Ulster that Royal Road ran
Through Lisburn, Lurgan, Portadown,
Solid British towns, lacking local grace.
Headscarved housewives in bulky floral skirts
Hugged market baskets on the plastic seats
Although it was near the borders of Tyrone —
End of the Pale, beginning of O'Neill —
Before a stranger turned a friendly face,
Yarning politics in Ulster monotone.
Bathos as we bumped all that twilight road,
Tales of the Ancient Order, Ulster's Volunteers:
Narrow fields wrought such division,
And narrow they were, though as darkness fell
Ruled by the evening star, which saw me home

To a gaunt farmhouse on this busy road,
Bisecting slopes of plaintive moorland,
Where I assume old ways of walk and work
So easily, yet feel the sadness of return
To what seems still, though changing.
No Wordsworthian dream enchants me here
With glint of glacial corrie, totemic mountain,
But merging low hills and gravel streams,
Oozy blackness of bog-banks, tough upland grass;
Rough Field in the Gaelic and rightly named
As setting for a mode of life that passes on:
Harsh landscape that haunts me,
Well and stone, in the bleak moors of dream,
With all my circling a failure to return.

5. LIKE DOLMENS ROUND MY CHILDHOOD

Like dolmens round my childhood, the old people.

Jamie MacCrystal sang to himself,
A broken song without tune, without words;
He tipped me a penny every pension day,
Fed kindly crusts to winter birds.
When he died his cottage was robbed,
Mattress and money-box torn and searched.
Only the corpse they didn't disturb.

Maggie Owens was surrounded by animals,
A mongrel bitch and shivering pups,
Even in her bedroom a she-goat cried.
She was a well of gossip defiled,
Fanged chronicler of a whole countryside;
Reputed a witch, all I could find
Was her lonely need to deride.

The Nialls lived along a mountain lane
Where heather bells bloomed, clumps of foxglove.
All were blind, with Blind Pension and Wireless.
Dead eyes serpent-flickered as one entered
To shelter from a downpour of mountain rain.
Crickets chirped under the rocking hearthstone
Until the muddy sun shone out again.

Mary Moore lived in a crumbling gatehouse,
Famous as Pisa for its leaning gable.
Bag-apron and boots, she tramped the fields
Driving lean cattle from a miry stable.
A byword for fierceness, she fell asleep
Over love stories, Red Star and Red Circle,
Dreamed of gypsy love-rites, by firelight sealed.

Wild Billy Eagleson married a Catholic servant girl
When all his Loyal family passed on:
We danced round him shouting 'To hell with King Billy',
And dodged from the arc of his flailing blackthorn.
Forsaken by both creeds, he showed little concern
Until the Orange drums banged past in the summer
And bowler and sash aggressively shone.

Curate and doctor trudged to attend them,
Through knee-deep snow, through summer heat,
From main road to lane to broken path,
Gulping the mountain air with painful breath.
Sometimes they were found by neighbours,
Silent keepers of a smokeless hearth,
Suddenly cast in the mould of death.

Ancient Ireland, indeed! I was reared by her bedside,
The rune and the chant, evil eye and averted head,

Fomorian fierceness of family and local feud.
Gaunt figures of fear and of friendliness,
For years they trespassed on my dreams
Until once, in a standing circle of stones,
I felt their shadows pass

Into that dark permanence of ancient forms.

II. The Leaping Fire

i.m. Brigid Montague (1876–1966)

Each morning, from the corner
of the hearth, I saw a miracle
as you sifted the smoored ashes
to blow
           a fire's sleeping remains
back to life, holding the burning brands
of turf, between work-hardened hands.
I draw on that fire...

I. THE LITTLE FLOWER'S DISCIPLE

Old lady, I now celebrate
to whom I owe so much;
bending over me in darkness
a scaly tenderness of touch

skin of bony arm & elbow
sandpapered with work:
because things be to be done
and simplicity did not shirk

the helpless, hopeless task
of maintaining a family farm,
which meant, by legal fiction,
maintaining a family name.

The thongless man's boots,
the shapeless bag-apron:
would your favourite saint
accept the harness of humiliation

you bore constantly until
the hiss of milk into the pail
became as lonely a prayer as
your vigil at the altar rail.

Roses showering from heaven
upon her uncorrupted body
after death, celebrated
the Little Flower's sanctity

& through the latticed grill
of your patron's enclosed order
an old French nun once threw me
a tiny sack of lavender.

So, from the pressed herbs
of your least memory, sweetness exudes:
that of the meek and the selfless,
who should be comforted.

2. THE LIVING & THE DEAD

Nightly she climbs
the narrow length of the stairs
to kneel in her cold room
as if she would storm
heaven with her prayers

which, if they have power,
now reach across the quiet
night of death to where
instead of a worn rosary,
I tell these metal keys.

The pain of a whole family
she gathers into her hands:
the spent mother who died
to give birth to children
scattered to the four winds

who now creakingly arouse
from darkness, distance
to populate the corners
of this silent house
they once knew so well.

A draught-whipped candle
magnifies her shadow —
a frail body grown monstrous,
sighing in a trance
before the gilt crucifix —

& as the light gutters
the shadows gather to dance
on the wall of the next room
where, a schoolboy searching sleep,
I begin to touch myself.

The sap of another generation
fingering through a broken tree
to push fresh branches
towards a further light,
a different identity.

3. OMAGH HOSPITAL

Your white hair
on the thin rack
of your shoulders

it is hard
to look into the eyes
of the dying

who carry away
a part of oneself—
a shared world

& you, whose life
was selflessness,
now die slowly

broken down by
process to a pale
exhausted beauty,

the moon in her
last phase, caring
only for herself.

I lean over
the bed but you barely
recognize me &

when an image
forces entry —
'Is that John?

Bring me home,'
you whimper &
I see a house

shaken by traffic
until a fault runs
from roof to base

but your face has
already retired into
the blind, animal

misery of age
paying out your
rosary beads,

hands twitching
as you drift
towards nothingness

4. A Hollow Note

Family legend held
that this frail
woman had heard
the banshee's wail

& on the night
she lay dying
I heard a low,
constant crying

over the indifferent
roofs of Paris —
the marsh bittern
or white owl sailing

from its foul
nest of bones
to warn me with
a hollow note

& among autobuses
& taxis, the shrill
paraphernalia of
a swollen city,

I crossed myself
from rusty habit
before I realized
why I had done it.

A hollow note...

FROM III. *The Bread God*

PENAL ROCK: ALTAMUSKIN

To learn the Mass rock's lesson, leave your car,
Descend frost-gripped steps to where
A humid moss overlaps the valley floor.
Crisp as a pistol-shot, the winter air
Recalls poor Tagues, folding the nap of their frieze
Under one knee, long suffering as beasts,
But parched for that surviving sign of grace,
The bog-Latin murmur of their priest.
A crude stone oratory, carved by a cousin,
Commemorates the place. For two hundred years
People of our name have sheltered in this glen
But now all have left. A few flowers
Wither on the altar, so I melt a ball of snow
From the hedge into their rusty tin before I go.

FROM IV. *A Severed Head*

2. A LOST TRADITION

All around, shards of a lost tradition:
From the Rough Field I went to school
In the Glen of the Hazels. Close by
Was the bishopric of the Golden Stone;
The cairn of Carleton's homesick poem.

Scattered over the hills, tribal-
And placenames, uncultivated pearls.
No rock or ruin, *dún* or dolmen
But showed memory defying cruelty
Through an image-encrusted name.

The heathery gap where the Rapparee,
Shane Barnagh, saw his brother die —
On a summer's day the dying sun
Stained its colours to crimson:
So breaks the heart, Brish-mo-Cree.

The whole landscape a manuscript
We had lost the skill to read,
A part of our past disinherited;
But fumbled, like a blind man,
Along the fingertips of instinct.

The last Gaelic speaker in the parish
When I stammered my school Irish
One Sunday after mass, crinkled
A rusty litany of praise:
Tá an Ghaeilge againn arís...*

Tír Eoghain: Land of Owen,
Province of the O'Niall;
The ghostly tread of O'Hagan's
Barefoot gallowglasses marching
To merge forces in Dún Geanainn

Push southward to Kinsale!
Loudly the war-cry is swallowed
In swirls of black rain and fog
As Ulster's pride, Elizabeth's foemen,
Founder in a Munster bog.

* *'We have the Irish again.'*

5. A Grafted Tongue

(Dumb,
bloodied, the severed
head now chokes to
speak another tongue—

As in
a long suppressed dream,
some stuttering garb-
led ordeal of my own)

An Irish
child weeps at school
repeating its English.
After each mistake

The master
gouges another mark
on the tally stick
hung about its neck

Like a bell
on a cow, a hobble
on a straying goat.
To slur and stumble

In shame
the altered syllables
of your own name;
to stray sadly home

And find
the turf-cured width
of your parents' hearth
growing slowly alien:

In cabin
and field they still
speak the old tongue.
You may greet no one.

To grow
a second tongue, as
harsh a humiliation
as twice to be born.

Decades later
that child's grandchild's
speech stumbles over lost
syllables of an old order.

FROM *V. The Fault*

2. THE SAME FAULT

When I am angry, sick or tired
A line on my forehead pulses,
The line on my left temple
Opened by an old car accident.
My father had the same scar
In the same place, as if
The same fault ran through
Us both: anger, impatience,
A stress born of violence.

3. SOUND OF A WOUND

Who knows
the sound a wound makes?
   Scar tissue
can rend, the old hurt
   tear open as
the torso of the fiddle
   groans to
carry the tune, to carry
   the pain of
a lost (slow herds of cattle
   roving over
soft meadow, dark bogland)
   pastoral rhythm.

I assert
a civilization died here;
   it trembles
underfoot where I walk these
   small, sad hills:
it rears in my bloodstream
   when I hear
a bleat of Saxon condescension,
   Westminster
to hell, it is less than these
   strangely carved
five-thousand-year resisting stones,
   that lonely cross.

This bitterness
I inherit from my father,
   the swarm of blood
to the brain, the vomit surge
   of race hatred,
the victim seeing the oppressor,

    bold Jacobean
planter, or gadget-laden marine,
    who has scattered
his household gods, used
    his people
as servants, flushed his women
    like game.

4. THE CAGE

My father, the least happy
man I have known. His face
retained the pallor
of those who work underground:
the lost years in Brooklyn
listening to a subway
shudder the earth.

But a traditional Irishman
who (released from his grille
in the Clark Street IRT)
drank neat whiskey until
he reached the only element
he felt at home in
any longer: brute oblivion.

And yet picked himself
up, most mornings,

to march down the street
extending his smile
to all sides of the good,
(all-white) neighbourhood
belled by St Teresa's Church.

When he came back
we walked together
across fields of Garvaghey
to see hawthorn on the summer
hedges, as though
he had never left;
a bend of the road

which still sheltered
primroses. But we
did not smile in
the shared complicity
of a dream, for when
weary Odysseus returns
Telemachus should leave.

Often as I descend
into subway or underground
I see his bald head behind
the bars of the small booth;
the mark of an old car
accident beating on his
ghostly forehead.

FROM *VI. A Good Night*

2. THE FIGHT

When I found the swallow's
Nest under the bridge —
Ankle-deep in the bog stream,
Traffic drumming overhead —
I was so pleased I ran
To fetch a school companion
To share the nude fragility
Of the shells, lightly freckled
With colour, in their cradle
Of feathers, twigs, earth.

It was still breast warm
Where I curved in my hand
To count them, one by one
Into his cold palm, a kind
Of trophy or offering. Turn-
Ing my back, to scoop out
The last, I heard him run
Down the echoing hollow
Of the bridge. Splashing
After, I bent tangled in
Bull wire at the bridge's
Mouth, when I saw him take
And break them, one by one
Against a sunlit stone.

For minutes we fought
Standing and falling in
The river's brown spate,
And I would still fight
Though now I can forgive.

To worship or destroy beauty—
That double edge of impulse
I recognize, by which we live;
But also the bitter paradox
Of betraying love to harm,
Then lungeing, too late,
With fists, to its defence.

4. THE SOURCE

Plan the next move. 'Whereabouts?
Don't forget the case of stout.'
Which only means that, dragging
A crate of bottles between us,
A rump parliament of old friends
Spend the lees of the night in
A mountain cottage, swapping
Stories, till cockcrow warns,
Then stagger home, drunk as coots,
Through the sleeping countryside.

A gate clangs, I grope against
A tent-fold of darkness until
Eye accepts the animal shape
Of the hedge, the sphere of
Speckled sky, the dim, damp
Fields breathing on either side.
The lane is smoothly tarred
Downhill to the humped bridge
Where I peer uncertainly over,
Lured towards sense by the
Unseen rattle of this mountain
Stream, whose lowland idlings
Define my townland's shape.

I climbed to its source once,
A journey perilous, through
The lifeless, lichened thorn
Of MacCrystal's Glen, a thread
Of water still leading me on
Past stale bog-cuttings, grey
Shapes slumped in rusty bracken,
Littered with fir's white bone:
Stranded mammoths! The water's
Thin music unwinding upwards
Till, high on a ledge of reeds
And heather, I came upon
A pool of ebony water
Fenced by rocks...

                    Legend
Declared a monster trout
Lived there, so I slipped
A hand under the fringe of
Each slick rock, splitting
The skin of turning froth
To find nothing but that
Wavering pulse leading to
The central heart where
The spring beat, so icy-cold
I shiver now in recollection,
Hearing its brisk, tireless
Movement over the pebbles
Beneath my feet...
                    Was that
The ancient trout of wisdom
I meant to catch? As I plod
Through the paling darkness
Details emerge, and memory

Warms. Old Danaghy raging
With his stick, to keep our
Cows from a well, that now
Is boarded up, like himself.
Here his son and I robbed a
Bee's nest, kicking the combs
Free; our boots smelt sweetly
For days afterwards. Snowdrop
In March, primrose in April,
Whitethorn in May, cardinal's
Fingers of foxglove dangling
All summer: every crevice held
A secret sweetness. Remembering,
I seem to smell wild honey
On my face.
          And plunge
Down the hillside, singing
In a mood of fierce elation.
My seven league boots devour
Time and space as I crash
Through the last pools of
Darkness. All around, my
Neighbours sleep, but I am
In possession of their past
(The pattern history weaves
From one small backward place)
Marching through memory magnified:
Each grassblade bends with
Translucent beads of moisture
And the bird of total meaning
Stirs upon its hidden branch.

As I reach the last lap
The seventh sense of drunkenness —

That extra pilot in the head —
Tells me I am being watched
And, wheeling, I confront a clump
Of bullocks. Inert in grass,
They gaze at me, saucer-eyed,
Turning their slow surprise
Upon their tongue. *Store cattle:*
The abattoirs of old England
Will soon put paid to them. In
A far meadow the corncrake
Turns its rusty ratchet and
I find myself rounding the
Last corner towards the black
Liquid gleam of the main road.

FROM *VII. Hymn to the New Omagh Road*

1. BALANCE SHEET

    I. Loss

Item: The shearing away of an old barn
        criss-cross of beams where pigeons moan
        high small window where the swallow built
        whitewashed drystone walls.

Item: The suppression of stone-lined paths
        old potato-boiler full of crocuses
        overhanging lilac or laburnum
        sweet pea climbing the fence.

Item: The filling-in of chance streams
        uncovered wells, all unchannelled sources

of water that might weaken foundations
bubbling over the macadam.

Item: The disappearance of all signs
of wild life, wren's or robin's nest
a rabbit nibbling a coltsfoot leaf
a stray squirrel or water rat.

Item: The uprooting of wayside hedges
with their accomplices, devil's bit and pee the bed
primrose and dog rose, an unlawful
assembly of thistles.

Item: The removal of all hillocks
and humps, superstition styled fairy forts
and long barrows, now legally to be regarded
as obstacles masking a driver's view.

2. Gain

Item: 10 men from the district being for a period of time fully em-
ployed, their 10 wives could buy groceries and clothes to send
30 children content to school for a few months, and raise local
merchants' hearts by paying their bills.

Item: A man driving from Belfast to Londonderry can arrive a quarter
of an hour earlier, a lorry load of goods ditto, thus making
Ulster more competitive in the international market.

Item: A local travelling from the prefabricated suburbs of by-passed
villages can manage an average of 50 rather than 40 mph on
his way to see relatives in Omagh hospital or lunatic asylum.

Item: The dead of Garvaghey Graveyard (including my grandfa-
ther) can have an unobstructed view — the trees having been

sheared away for a carpark — of the living passing at great
speed, sometimes quick enough to come straight in:

> Let it be clear
> That I do not grudge my grandfather
> This long delayed pleasure!
> I like the idea of him
> Rising from the rotting boards of the coffin
> With his JP's white beard
> And penalizing drivers
> For travelling faster
> Than jaunting cars.

FROM **VIII. *Patriotic Suite***

9. THE SIEGE OF MULLINGAR

At the Fleadh Cheoil in Mullingar
There were two sounds, the breaking
Of glass, and the background pulse
Of music. Young girls roamed
The streets with eager faces,
Shoving for men. Bottles in
Hand, they rowed out a song:
*Puritan Ireland's dead and gone,
A myth of O'Connor and Ó Faoláin.*

In the early morning the lovers
Lay on both sides of the canal
Listening on Sony transistors
To the agony of Pope John.
Yet it didn't seem strange or blasphemous,
This ground bass of death and

Resurrection, as we strolled along:
Puritan Ireland's dead and gone,
A myth of O'Connor and Ó Faoláin.

Further on, breasting the wind
Waves of the deserted grain harbour,
A silent pair, a cob and his pen,
Most nobly linked. Everything then
In our casual morning vision
Seemed to flow in one direction,
Lines simple as a song:
Puritan Ireland's dead and gone,
A myth of O'Connor and Ó Faoláin.

X. The Wild Dog Rose

i.m. *Minnie Kearney*

1.

I go to say goodbye to the *cailleach,*
that terrible figure who haunted my childhood
but no longer harsh, a human being
merely, hurt by event.
                              The cottage,
circled by trees, weathered to admonitory
shapes of desolation by the mountain winds,
straggles into view. The rank thistles
and leathery bracken of untilled fields
stretch behind with — a final outcrop —
the hooped figure by the roadside,
its retinue of dogs
                              which give tongue
as I approach, with savage, whingeing cries

so that she slowly turns, a moving nest
of shawls and rags, to view, to stare
the stranger down.
                          And I feel again
that ancient awe, the terror of a child
before the great hooked nose, the cheeks
dewlapped with dirt, the staring blue
of the sunken eyes, the mottled claws
clutching a stick
                          but now hold
and return her gaze, to greet her,
as she greets me, in friendliness.
Memories have wrought reconciliation
between us, we talk in ease at last,
like old friends, lovers almost,
sharing secrets
                          of neighbours
she quarrelled with, who now lie
in Garvaghey graveyard, beyond all hatred;
of my family and hers, how she never married,
though a man came asking in her youth.
'You would be loath to leave your own,'
she sighs, 'and go among strangers'—
his parish ten miles off.
                          For sixty years
since, she has lived alone, in one place.
Obscurely honoured by such confidences,
I idle by the summer roadside, listening,
while the monologue falters, continues,
rehearsing the small events of her life.
The only true madness is loneliness,
the monotonous voice in the skull
that never stops
                          because never heard.

2.

And there
where the dog rose shines in the hedge
she tells me a story so terrible
that I try to push it away,
my bones melting.
                Late at night
a drunk came beating at her door
to break it in, the bolt snapping
from the soft wood, the thin mongrels
rushing to cut but yelping as
he whirls with his farm boots
to crush their skulls.
                    In the darkness
they wrestle, two creatures crazed
with loneliness, the smell of the
decaying cottage in his nostrils
like a drug, his body heavy on hers,
the tasteless trunk of a seventy-year-
old virgin, which he rummages while
she battles for life
                  bony fingers
reaching desperately to push
against his bull neck. 'I prayed
to the Blessed Virgin herself
for help and after a time
I broke his grip.'
              He rolls
to the floor, snores asleep,
while she cowers until dawn
and the dogs' whimpering starts
him awake, to lurch back across
the wet bog.

3.

        And still
the dog rose shines in the hedge.
Petals beaten wide by rain, it
sways slightly, at the tip of a
slender, tangled, arching branch
which, with her stick, she gathers
into us.
        'The wild rose
is the only rose without thorns,'
she says, holding a wet blossom
for a second, in a hand knotted
as the knob of her stick.
'Whenever I see it, I remember
the Holy Mother of God and
all she suffered.'
        Briefly
the air is strong with the smell
of that weak flower, offering
its crumbling yellow cup
and pale bleeding lips
fading to white
        at the rim
of each bruised and heart-
shaped petal.

Epilogue

Driving South, we pass through Cavan,
lakeside orchards in first bloom,
hawthorn with a surplice whiteness,
binding the small holdings of Monaghan.

A changing rural pattern means clack
of tractor for horse, sentinel shape
of silo, hum of milking machine:
the same from Ulster to the Ukraine.

Only a sentimentalist would wish
to see such degradation again:
heavy tasks from spring to harvest;
the sackcloth pilgrimages under rain

to repair the slabbery gaps of winter
with the labourer hibernating
in his cottage for half the year
to greet the indignity of the Hiring Fair.

Fewer hands, bigger markets, larger farms.
Yet something mourns. The iron-ribbed
lamp flitting through the yard at dark,
the hissing froth, and fodder-scented warmth

of a wood-stalled byre, or leather thong
of flail curling in a barn, were part
of a world where action had been wrung
through painstaking years to ritual.

Acknowledged when the priest blessed
the green-tipped corn, or Protestant
lugged thick turnip, swollen marrow
to robe the kirk for Thanksgiving.

Palmer's softly lit Vale of Shoreham
commemorates it, or Chagall's lovers
floating above a childhood village
remote but friendly as Goldsmith's Auburn—

Our finally lost dream of man at home
in a rural setting! A giant hand,
as we pass by, reaches down
to grasp the fields we gazed upon.

Harsh landscape that haunts me,
well and stone, in the bleak moors of dream
with all my circling a failure to return
to what is already going
                    going
                         GONE

from

A SLOW DANCE

(1975)

1. *Sweeney*

A wet silence.
Wait under trees,
muscles tense,
ear lifted, eye alert.

Lungs clear.
A nest of senses
stirring awake —
human beast!

A bird lights:
two claw prints.
Two leaves shift:
a small wind.

Beneath, white
rush of current,
stone chattering
between high banks.

Occasional shrill
of a bird, squirrel
trampolining along
a springy branch.

Start a slow
dance, lifting
a foot, planting
a heel to celebrate

greenness, rain
spatter on skin,
the humid pull
of the earth.

The whole world
turning in wet
and silence, a
damp mill wheel.

2. The Dance

In silence and isolation the dance begins. No one is meant to watch,
least of all yourself. Hands fall to the sides, the head lolls, empty, a
broken stalk. The shoes fall away from the feet, the clothes peel away
from the skin, body rags. The sight has slowly faded from your eyes,
that sight of habit which sees nothing. Your ears buzz a little before
they retreat to where the heart pulses, a soft drum. Then the dance
begins, cleansing, healing. Through the bare forehead, along the
bones of the feet, the earth begins to speak. One knee lifts rustily,
then the other. Totally absent, you shuffle up and down, the purse of
your loins striking against your thighs, sperm and urine oozing down
your lower body like a gum. From where the legs join the rhythm
spreads upwards — the branch of the penis lifting, the cage of the ribs
whistling — to pass down the arms like electricity along a wire. On
the skin moisture forms, a wet leaf or a windbreath light as a mayfly.
In wet and darkness you are reborn, the rain falling on your face as
it would on a mossy tree trunk, wet hair clinging to your skull like
bark, your breath mingling with the exhalations of the earth, that
eternal smell of humus and mould.

3. *Message*

With a body
heavy as earth
she begins to speak;

her words
are dew, bright,
deadly to drink,

her hair,
the damp mare's
nest of the grass

her arms,
thighs, chance
of a swaying branch

her secret
message, shaped
by a wandering wind

puts the eye
of reason out;
so novice, blind,

ease your
hand into the
rot-smelling crotch

of a hollow
tree, and find
two pebbles of quartz

protected by
a spider's web:
her sunless breasts.

4. *Seskilgreen*

A circle of stones
surviving behind
a guttery farmhouse,

the capstone phallic
in a thistly meadow:
Seskilgreen Passage Grave.

Cup, circle,
triangle beating
their secret dance

(eyes, breasts,
thighs of a still
fragrant goddess).

I came last in May
to find the mound
drowned in bluebells

with a fearless wren
hoarding speckled eggs
in a stony crevice

while cattle
swayed sleepily
under low branches

lashing the ropes
of their tails
across the centuries.

5. For the Hillmother

Hinge of silence
   creak for us
Rose of darkness
   unfold for us
Wood anemone
   sway for us
Blue harebell
   bend to us
Moist fern
   unfurl for us
Springy moss
   uphold us
Branch of pleasure
   lean on us
Leaves of delight
   murmur for us
Odorous wood
   breathe on us
Evening dews
   pearl for us
Freshet of ease
   flow for us
Secret waterfall
   pour for us
Hidden cleft
   speak to us
Portal of delight
   inflame us
Hill of motherhood
   wait for us
Gate of birth
   open for us

Courtyard in Winter

Snow curls in on the cold wind.

Slowly I push back the door.
After long absence old habits
Are painfully revived, those disciplines
Which enable us to survive,
To keep a minimal fury alive
While flake by faltering flake

Snow curls in on the cold wind.

Along the courtyard the boss
Of each cobblestone is rimmed
In white, with winter's weight
Pressing, like a silver shield,
On all the small plots of earth,
Inert in their living death as

Snow curls in on the cold wind.

Seized in a giant fist of frost
The grounded planes at London Airport,
Mallarmé swans trapped in ice.
The friend whom I have just left
Will be dead, a year from now,
Through her own fault, while

Snow curls in on the cold wind.

Or smothered by some glacial truth?
Thirty years ago I learnt to reach
Across the rusting hoops of steel

That bound our greening waterbarrel
To save the living water beneath
The hardening crust of ice, before

Snow curls in on the cold wind.

But despair has a deeper crust.
In all our hours together I never
Managed to ease the single hurt
That edged her towards her death,
Never reached through her loneliness
To save a trust, chilled after

Snow curls in on the cold wind.

I plunged through snowdrifts once,
Above our home, to carry
A telegram to a mountain farm.
Fearful but inviting, they waved me
To warm myself at the flaring
Hearth before I faced again where

Snow curls in on the cold wind.

The news I brought was sadness.
In a far city someone of their name
Lay dying. The tracks of foxes,
Wild birds, as I climbed down
Seemed to form a secret writing
Minute and frail as life when

Snow curls in on the cold wind.

Sometimes I know that message.
There is a disease called snow-sickness;
The glare from the bright god,

The earth's reply. As if that
Ceaseless, glittering light was
All the truth we'd left after

Snow curls in on the cold wind.

So, before dawn, comfort fails.
I imagine her end, in some sad
Bedsitting room, the steady hiss
Of the gas more welcome than an
Act of friendship, the protective
Oblivion of a lover's caress if

Snow curls in on the cold wind.

In the canyon of the street
The dark snowclouds hesitate,
Turning to slush almost before
They cross the taut canvas of
The street stalls, the bustle
Of a sweeper's brush after

Snow curls in on the cold wind.

The walls are spectral, white.
All the trees black-ribbed, bare.
Only veins of ivy, the sturdy
Laurel with its waxen leaves,
Its scant dark berries, survive
To form a winter wreath as

Snow curls in on the cold wind.

What solace but endurance, kindness?
Against her choice, I still affirm
That nothing dies, that even from

Such bitter failure memory grows;
The snowflake's structure, fragile
But intricate as the rose when

Snow curls in on the cold wind.

Dowager

I dwell in this leaky Western castle.
American matrons weave across the carpet,
Sorefooted as camels, and less useful.

Smooth Ionic columns hold up a roof.
A chandelier shines on a foxhound's coat:
The grandson of a grandmother I reared.

In the old days I read or embroidered,
But now it is enough to see the sky change,
Clouds extend or smother a mountain's shape.

Wet afternoons I ride in the Rolls;
Windshield wipers flail helpless against the rain:
I thrash through pools like smashing panes of glass.

And the light afterwards! Hedges steam,
I ride through a damp tunnel of sweetness,
The bonnet strewn with bridal hawthorn

From which a silver lady leaps, always young.
Alone, I hum with satisfaction in the sun,
An old bitch, with a warm mouthful of game.

The Errigal Road

We match paces along the Hill Head Road,
the road to the old churchyard of Errigal Keerogue;
its early cross, a heavy stone hidden in grass.

As we climb my old Protestant neighbour
signals landmarks along his well-trodden path,
some hill or valley celebrated in local myth.

'Yonder's Whiskey Hollow,' he declares,
indicating a line of lunar birches.
We halt to imagine men plotting

against the wind, feeding the fire or
smothering the fumes of an old-fashioned worm
while the secret liquid bubbles & clears.

'And that's Foxhole Brae under there —'
pointing to the torn face of a quarry.
'It used to be crawling with them.'

(A red quarry slinks through the heather,
a movement swift as a bird's, melting as rain,
glimpsed behind a mound, disappears again.)

At Fairy Thorn Height the view fans out,
ruck and rise to where, swathed in mist
& rain, swells the mysterious saddle shape

of Knockmany Hill, its brooding tumulus
opening perspectives beyond our Christian myth.
'On a clear day you can see far into Monaghan,'

old Eagleson says, and we exchange sad notes
about the violence plaguing these parts;
last week, a gun battle outside Aughnacloy,

machine-gun fire splintering the wet thorns,
two men beaten up near dark Altamuskin,
an attempt to blow up Omagh Courthouse.

Helicopters overhead, hovering locusts.
Heavily booted soldiers probing vehicles, streets,
their strange antennae bristling, like insects.

At his lane's end, he turns to face me.
'Tell them down South that old neighbours
can still speak to each other around here'

& gives me his hand, but does not ask me in.
Rain misting my coat, I turn back towards
the main road, where cars whip smartly past

between small farms, fading back into forest.
Soon all our shared landscape will be effaced,
a quick stubble of pine recovering most.

Windharp

for Patrick Collins

The sounds of Ireland,
that restless whispering
you never get away
from, seeping out of

low bushes and grass,
heatherbells and fern,
wrinkling bog pools,
scraping tree branches,
light hunting cloud,
sound hounding sight,
a hand ceaselessly
combing and stroking
the landscape, till
the valley gleams
like the pile upon
a mountain pony's coat.

FROM *The Cave of Night*

3. CAVE

The rifled honeycomb
of the high-rise hotel
where a wind tunnel moans.
While jungle-clad troops
ransack the Falls, race
through huddled streets,
we lie awake, the wide
window washed with rain,
your oval face and tide
of yellow hair luminous
as you turn to me again
seeking refuge as the
cave of night blooms
with fresh explosions.

5. FALLS FUNERAL

Unmarked faces
fierce with grief

a line of children
led by a small coffin

the young
mourning the young

a sight beyond tears
beyond pious belief

David's brethren
in the Land of Goliath.

6. RATONNADE

Godoi, godoi, godoi!
Our city burns & so did Troy,
Finic, Finic, marsh birds cry
As bricks assemble a new toy.

    Godoi, godoi, godoi.

Humble mousewives crouch in caves,
Monster rats lash their tails,
Cheese grows scarce in Kingdom Come,
Rodents leap to sound of drum.

    Godoi, godoi, godoi.

Civilization slips & slides when
Death sails past with ballroom glide:
Tangomaster of the skulls whose
Harvest lies in griefs & rues.

Godoi, godoi, godoi.

On small hillsides darkens fire,
Wheel goes up, forgetting tyre,
Grudgery holds its winter court,
Smash and smithereens to report.

Godoi, godoi, godoi.

Against such horrors hold a cry,
Sweetness mothers us to die,
Wisens digs his garden patch,
Silence lifts a silver latch.

Godoi, godoi, godoi.

Mingle musk, love-birds say,
Honey-hiving all the day,
Ears & lips & private parts,
Muffled as the sound of carts.

Godoi, godoi, godoi.

Moral is of worsening hours,
Cripple twisting only flowers,
One arm lost, one leg found,
Sad men fall on common ground.

Godoi!

Killing the Pig

The noise.

He was pulled out, squealing,
an iron cleek sunk in the roof
of his mouth.

(Don't say they are not intelligent:
they know the hour has come
and they want none of it;
they dig in their little trotters,

will not go dumb or singing
to the slaughter.)

That high-pitched final effort,
no single sound could match it —
a big plane roaring off,
a diva soaring towards her last note,
the brain-chilling persistence of an electric saw,
scrap being crushed.

Piercing & absolute,
only high heaven ignores it.

Then a full stop.
Mickey Boyle plants
a solid thump of the mallet
flat between the ears.

Swiftly the knife seeks the throat;
swiftly the other cleavers work
till the carcass is hung up
shining and eviscerated as
a surgeon's coat.

A child is given
the bladder to play with.
But the walls of the farmyard
still hold that scream,
are built around it.

The Massacre

Two crows flap to a winter wood.
Soldiers with lances and swords
Probe the entrails of innocents.
A burgomaster washes manicured
Hands before mourning citizens.
The snow on the gable is linen crisp,
That on the ground laced with blood.
Two crows flap to a winter wood.

A Graveyard in Queens

for Eileen Carney

We hesitate along
flower-encumbered

avenues of the dead;
Greek, Puerto-Rican,

Italian, Irish —
(our true Catholic

world, a graveyard)
but a squirrel

dances us to it
through the water-

sprinklered grass,
collapsing wreaths,

& taller than you
by half, lately from

that hidden village
where you were born

I sway with you
in a sad, awkward

dance of pain
over the grave of

my uncle & namesake —
the country fiddler —

& the grave of almost
all your life held,

your husband & son
all three sheltering

under the same
squat, grey stone.

*

You would cry out
against what has

happened, such
heedless hurt,

had you the harsh
nature for it

(swelling the North
wind with groans,

curses, imprecations
against heaven's will)

but your mind is
a humble house, a

soft light burning
beneath the holy

picture, the image
of the seven times

wounded heart of
her, whose portion

is to endure. For
there is no end

to pain, nor of
love to match it

& I remember Anne
meekest of my aunts

rocking and praying
in her empty room.

Oh, the absurdity
of grief in that

doll's house, all
the chair legs sawn

to nurse dead children:
love's museum!

*

It sent me down
to the millstream

to spy upon a
mournful waterhen

shushing her young
along the autumn

flood, as seriously
as a policeman and

after scampering
along, the proud

plumed squirrel
now halts, to stand

at the border
of this grave plot

serious, still,
a small ornament

holding something,
a nut, a leaf—

like an offering
inside its paws.

*

For an instant
you smile to see

his antics, then
bend to tidy

flowers, gravel,
like any woman

making a bed,
arranging a room,

over what were
your darlings' heads

and far from
our supposed home

I submit again
to stare soberly

at my own name
cut on a gravestone

& hear the creak
of a ghostly fiddle

filter through
American earth

the slow pride
of a lament.

from

THE GREAT CLOAK

(1978)

TRACKS

1.

The vast bedroom
a hall of air,
our linked bodies
lying there.

2.

As I turn to kiss
your long, black
hair, small breasts,
heat flares from
your fragrant skin,
your eyes widen as
deeper, more certain
and often, I enter
to search possession
of where your being
hides in flesh.

3.

Behind our eyelids
a landscape opens,
a violet horizon
pilgrims labour across,
a sky of colours
that change, explode

a fantail of stars,
the mental lightning
of sex illuminating
the walls of the skull;
a floating pleasure dome.

4.

I shall miss you
creaks the mirror
into which the scene
shortly disappears:
the vast bedroom
a hall of air, the
tracks of our bodies
fading there, while
giggling maids push
a trolley of fresh
linen down the corridor.

CAUGHT

A slight girl and easily got rid of:
He took his pleasure in an idle dance,
Laughed to hear her cry under him,
But woke to find his body in a trance.
Wherever he walked he seemed to see
Her approaching figure, whoever spoke
He strained for echoes of her voice
And, in a rage of loss, turned back
To where she slept, hands clasped on

Small breasts in a posture of defence.
Conqueror turned plaintiff, he tries
To uncurl them, to see long-lashed eyes
Turn slowly up, hear a meek voice say:
'Are you back, my love, back to stay?'

CLOSED CIRCUIT

An ache, anger
thunder of a hurtling
waterfall in the ears:
in abrupt detail he sees
the room where she lays
her pale, soft body
under another's

her petal mouth
raised to absorb
his probing kiss
and hears her small voice
cry animal cries
in the hissing anguish
the release of

my sweet one
my darling, my love
until they fall apart
(Oh, the merciless creak
of jealousy's film)
in a wet calm
like flowers after rain.

Talisman

After talking together
we move, as by a natural
progress, to make love.
Slant afternoon light

on the bed, the unlatched
window, scattered sheets
are part of a pattern
hastening towards memory

as you give yourself
to me with a cry of
joy, not hunger, while
I receive the gift

in ease, not raw desire
& all the superstructure
of the city outside —
twenty iron floors

of hotel dropping
to where the late sun
strikes the shield of
the lake, its chill towers —

elements in a slowly
developing dream, a talisman
of calm, to invoke against
unease, to invoke against harm.

DON JUAN'S FAREWELL

Ladies I have lain
    with in darkened rooms
sweet shudder of flesh
    behind shadowy blinds
long bars of light
    across tipped breasts
young flesh redolent
    of crumpled roses
the tender anxiety
    of the middle-aged
a hovering candle
    hiding blue veins
eloquent exhaustion
    watching light fade
as your drowsy partner
    drifts towards the
warm shores of sleep
    and you slowly awake
to confront again
    the alluring lie
of searching through
    another's pliant body
for something missing
    in your separate self
while profound night
    like a black swan
goes pluming past.

TEARING

1.

I sing your pain
as best I can
   seek
like a gentle man
   to assume
the proffered blame.

But the pose breaks.
The sour facts remain.
   It takes two
to make, or break
   a marriage.
Unhood the falcon!

2. *Pastourelle*

Hands on the pommel,
long dress trailing
over polished leather
riding boots, a spur
jutting from the heel,
& beneath, the bridle path,
strewn with rusty apples,
brown knobs of chestnut,
meadow saffron and acorn.

Then we were in the high
ribbed dark of the trees
where animals move stealth-
ily, coupling & killing,

while we talked nostalgically
of our lives, bedevilled
& betrayed by lost love —
the furious mole, tunnelling
near us his tiny kingdom —

& how slowly we had come
to where we wished each other
happiness, far and apart, as
a hawk circled the wood,
& a victim cried, the sound
of hooves rising & falling
upon bramble & fern, while
a thin growth of rain gathers
about us, like a cowl.

3. Never

In the gathering dark
I caress your head
as you thrash out
flat words of pain:
'There is no way back,
I can feel it happening;
we shall never be
what we were, again.'

Never, a solemn bell
tolling through
that darkening room
where I cradle your head,
only a glimmer left
in the high window
over what was once
our marriage bed.

4. *Refrain*

I sit in autumn sunlight
on a hotel terrace as I did

when our marriage had begun,
our public honeymoon,

try to unsnarl what went wrong,
shouldering all the blame,

but no chivalric mode,
courtesy's silent discipline

softens the pain
when something is ending

and the tearing begins:
'We shall never be

what we were, again.'
Old love's refrain.

SHE WALKS ALONE

In the white city of Evora, absence accosted me.
You were reading in bed, while I walked all night alone.
Were you worried about me, or drifting towards sleep?

I saw the temple of Diana, bone-white in the moonlight.
I made a private prayer to her, for strength to continue:
Not since convent days have I prayed so earnestly.

A dog came out of the shadows, brushed against my leg.
He followed me everywhere, pushing his nose into my hand.
Soon the cats appeared, little scraggy bundles of need.

There were more monuments, vivid as hallucinations.
Suddenly, a young man stepped out of the shadows:
I was not terrified, as I might have been at home.

Besides, he was smiling & gentle as you used to be.
'A kiss,' he pleads 'a kiss,' in soft Portuguese.
I quickened my step, but he padded behind me.

He looked so young, my heart went out to him.
I stopped in the shadows under the Cathedral.
We kissed, and the tears scalded my face.

No Music

I'll tell you a sore truth, little understood.
It's harder to leave, than to be left:
To stay, to leave, both sting wrong.

You will always have me to blame,
Can dream we might have sailed on;
From absence's rib, a warm fiction.

But I must recognize what I have done
And, if it fails, accept the burden
Of the harm done to you & another one.

To tear up old love by the roots,
To trample on past affections:
There is no music for so harsh a song.

The Blue Room

Tired, turning, restless,
the insomniac feels the pulse
that feeds his body

pity for his past,
fear of the future,
his spirit beats

along his veins
a ceaseless, dervish dance
which defies oblivion.

Night a pit into
which he falls & falls
endlessly, his memories

a circle of hobbyhorses
grinding up and down
gross, grinning teeth

until dawn biting
its throat, a bird
starts its habitual,

terrible, day-beginning cry.
The trees emerge from the stillness.
The raindrop bends the leaf.

HERBERT STREET REVISITED

for Madeleine

1.

A light is burning late
in this Georgian Dublin street:
someone is leading our old lives!

And our black cat scampers again
through the wet grass of the convent garden
upon his masculine errands.

The pubs shut: a released bull,
Behan shoulders up the street,
topples into our basement, roaring 'John!'

A pony and donkey cropped flank
by flank under the trees opposite;
short neck up, long neck down,

as Nurse Mullen knelt by her bedside
to pray for her lost Mayo hills,
the bruised bodies of Easter Volunteers.

Animals, neighbours, treading the pattern
of one time and place into history,
like our early marriage, while

tall windows looked down upon us
from walls flushed light pink or salmon
watching and enduring succession.

2.

As I leave you whisper,
'Don't betray our truth,'
and, like a ghost dancer
invoking a lost tribal strength,
I halt in tree-fed darkness
to summon back our past,
and celebrate a love that eased
so kindly, the dying bone,
enabling the spirit to sing
of old happiness, when alone.

3.

So put the leaves back on the tree,
put the tree back in the ground,
let Brendan trundle his corpse down
the street singing, like Molly Malone.

Let the black cat, tiny emissary
of our happiness, streak again
through the darkness, to fall soft-
clawed into a landlord's dustbin.

Let Nurse Mullen take the last
train to Westport, and die upright
in her chair, facing a window
warm with the blue slopes of Nephin.

And let the pony and donkey come —
look, someone has left the gate open —
like hobbyhorses linked in
the slow motion of a dream

parading side by side, down
the length of Herbert Street,
rising and falling, lifting
their hooves through the moonlight.

from III. *Anchor*

A Meeting

from the Irish, 9th century

The son of the King of the Moy
met a girl in green woods on midsummer's day:
she gave him black fruit from thorns
& the full of his arms
of strawberries, where they lay.

The Same Gesture

There is a secret room
of golden light where
everything — love, violence,
hatred is possible;
and, again, love.

Such intimacy of hand
and mind is achieved
under its healing light
that the shifting of
hands is a rite

like court music.
We barely know our

selves there though
it is what we always were—
most nakedly are—

and must remember
when we leave, re-
suming our habits
with our clothes:
work, phone, drive

through late traffic
changing gears with
the same gesture as
eased your snowbound
heart and flesh.

BLESSING

A feel of warmth in this place.
In winter air a scent of harvest.
No form of prayer is needed
When by sudden grace attended.
Naturally, we fall from grace.
Mere humans, we forget what light
Led us, lonely, to this place.

SUNSET

from the Féliré Aengus

In Lough Leane
a queen went swimming;
a redgold salmon
flowed into her
at full of evening.

CHILD

for Oonagh

A firefly gleams, then
fades upon your cheek.
Now you hide beneath
everything I write;
love's invisible ink,
heart's watermark.

THE POINT

Rocks jagged in morning mist.
At intervals the foghorn sounds
From the white lighthouse rock,
Lonely as cow mourning her calf,
Groaning, belly deep, desperate.

I assisted at such failure once;
A night-long fight to save a calf
Born finally, with broken neck.
It flailed briefly on the straw,
A wide-eyed mother straddling it.

But this is different.
It sounds to guide, not lament.
When the defining light is powerless,
Ships hesitating down the strait
Hear its harsh voice as friendliness.

Upstairs my wife & daughter sleep.
Our two lives have separated now
But I would send my voice to yours
Cutting through the shrouding mist
Like some friendly signal in distress.

The fog is lifting, slowly.
Flag high a new ship is entering.
The opposite shore unveils itself,
Bright in detail as a painting,
Alone, but equal to the morning.

EDGE

To fly into risk,
attempt the dream,
cast off, as we have done,
requires true luck

who know ourselves
blessed to have found
between this harbour's arms
a sheltering home

where the vast
tides of the Atlantic
lift to caress
rose-coloured rocks.

So fate relents.
Hushed and calm,
safe and secret,
on the edge is best.

from

THE DEAD KINGDOM

(1984)

PROCESS

The structure of process,
time's gullet devouring
parents whose children
are swallowed in turn,
families, houses, towns,
built or battered down,
only the earth and sky
unchanging in change,
everything else fragile
as a wild bird's wing;
bulldozer and butterfly,
dog rose and snowflake
climb the unending stair
into God's golden eye.

Each close in his own
world of sense & memory,
races, nations locked
in their dream of history,
only love or friendship,
an absorbing discipline
(the healing harmony
of music, painting, poem)
as swaying rope ladders
across fuming oblivion
while the globe turns,
and the stars turn, and
the great circles shine,
gold & silver,

    sun & moon.

THE MUSIC BOX

And now, the road towards Cavan.
Each year we left you down
by the roadside, Mary Mulvey,
to seek out old relations.
We waited as you hobbled
away up that summer boreen.

Mary lived in the leaning
cottage beside the old well
she strove to keep clean,
bending to skin dead leaves
and insects; ageing guardian
whom we found so frightening

Huddled on the leather seats
of Uncle John's Tin Lizzie,
away from your sour, black
shawls, clacking rosary, not
your bag of peppermints, which
we devoured thoughtlessly.

'Maria Marunkey', our hurtful
childish name for your strange
shape, suffering age, its shame
that hooped your back, cramped
and horrible as some toothy witch.
We clattered stones on your roof

Or hunkered whispering past
your half-door, malefic dwarfs,
to startle your curtained silence
with shouts, coarse as farts:

'Maria Marunkey married a donkey.'
The latch stirs; we scatter, bravely.

Blessedly, you could barely hear,
or begged us in, with further sweets
or gifts, to share your secret.
Nudging, we thronged around
as you laboriously wound —
more creakingly each year —

The magic music box, resurrected
from camphored lace, which ground
out such light, regular sounds,
thawing ice, tinkling raindrops,
a small figure on its rosewood top
twirling slowly, tireless dancer.

By its grace I still remember
you, Mary Mulvey, hobbling along
a summer lane, bent over the well
or shuffling into your cottage,
its gable sideways, like yourself.
Your visits to the home place

To see old friends and neighbours
stopped one year when you were
too crippled to move, and besides,
'There's no one left up there.
They've all died off.' A silver
dancer stops. Silent. Motionless.

THE WELL DREAMS

1.

The well dreams;
liquid bubbles.

Or it stirs
as a water spider skitters across;
a skinny-legged dancer.

Sometimes, a gross interruption;
a stone plumps in.
That takes a while to absorb,
to digest, much groaning
and commotion in the well's stomach
before it can proffer again
an almost sleek surface.

Even a pebble disturbs
that tremor-laden meniscus,
that implicit shivering.
They sink towards the floor,
the basement of quiet,
settle into a small mosaic.

And the single eye
of the well dreams on,
a silent cyclops.

2.

People are different.
They live outside, insist
in their world of agitation.
A man comes by himself,
singing or in silence,
and hauls up his bucket slowly —
an act of meditation —
or jerks it up angrily,
like lifting a skin,
sweeping a circle
right through his own reflection.

3.

And the well recomposes itself.

Crowds arrive annually, on pilgrimage.
Votive offerings adorn the bushes;
a child's rattle, hanging silent
(except when the wind shifts it),
a rag fluttering like a pennant.

Or a tarnished coin is thrown in,
sinking soundlessly to the bottom.
Water's slow alchemy washes it clean:
a queen of the realm, made virgin again.

4.

Birds chatter above it.
They are the well's principal distraction,

swaying at the end of branches,
singing and swaying, darting excitement
of courting and nesting,
fending for the next brood,
who still seem the same robin,
thrush, blackbird or wren.

The trees stay silent.
The storms speak through them.
Then the leaves come sailing down,
sharp green or yellow,
betraying the seasons,
till a flashing shield of ice
forms over the well's single eye:
the year's final gift,
a static transparence.

5.

But a well has its secret.
Under drifting leaves,
dormant stones around
the whitewashed wall,
the unpredictable ballet
of waterbugs, insects,

There the wellhead pulses,
little more than a tremor,
a flickering quiver,
spasms of silence;
small intensities of mirth,
the hidden laughter of earth.

RED BRANCH (*A Blessing*)

Sing a song for the broken
towns of old Tyrone:
Omagh, Dungannon, Strabane,
jagged walls and windows,
slowly falling down.

Sing a song for the homes
or owners that were here today
and tomorrow are gone;
Irish Street in Dungannon,
my friend Jim Devlin.

Sing a song for the people,
so grimly holding on,
Protestant and Catholic, fingered
at teabreak, shot inside their home:
the iron circle of retaliation.

Sing a song for the creaking branch
they find themselves upon,
hollow from top to bottom,
the stricken limb of Ulster,
slowly blown down.

Sing an end to sectarianism,
Fenian and Free Presbyterian,
the punishment slowly grown
more monstrous than the crime,
an enormous seeping bloodstain.

Sing our forlorn hope then —
the great Cross of Verdun,
Belfast's Tower on the Somme —
signs raised over bloody ground
that two crazed peoples make an end.

FROM   IV. *The Silver Flask*

AT LAST

A small sad man with a hat,
he came through the Customs at Cobh
carrying a roped suitcase and
something in me began to contract

but also to expand. We stood,
his grown sons, seeking for words
which under the clouding mist
turn to clumsy, laughing gestures.

At the mouth of the harbour lay
the squat shape of the liner
hooting farewell, with the waves
striking against Spike Island's grey.

We drove across Ireland that day,
lush river valleys of Cork, russet
of the Central Plain, landscapes
exotic to us Northerners, halting

only in a snug beyond Athlone
to hear a broadcast I had done.

How strange in that cramped room
my disembodied voice, the silence

after, as we looked at each other!
Slowly our eyes managed recognition.
'Not bad,' he said, and raised his glass:
Father and son at ease, at last.

The Silver Flask

Sweet, though short, our
hours as a family together.
Driving across dark mountains
to Midnight Mass in Fivemiletown,
lights coming up in the valleys
as in the days of Carleton.

Tussocks of heather brown
in the headlights; our mother
stowed in the back, a tartan
rug wrapped round her knees,
patiently listening as Father sang,
and the silver flask went round.

Chorus after chorus of the 'Adoremus'
to shorten the road before us,
till *we see amidst the winter's snows*
the festive lights of the small town
and from the choirloft an organ booms
angels we have heard on high, with

my father joining warmly in,
his broken tenor soaring, faltering,
a legend in dim bars of Brooklyn

(that sacramental moment of stillness
among exiled, disgruntled men)
now raised vehemently once again

in the valleys he had sprung from,
startling the stiff congregation
with fierce blasts of song, while
our mother sat silent beside him,
sad but proud, an unaccustomed
blush mantling her wan countenance.

Then driving slowly home,
tongues crossed with the Communion
wafer, snowflakes melting in
the car's hungry headlights,
till we reach the warm kitchen
and the spirits round again.

The family circle briefly restored
nearly twenty lonely years after
that last Christmas in Brooklyn,
under the same tinsel of decorations
so carefully hoarded by our mother
in the cabin trunk of a Cunard liner.

Last Journey

i.m. James Montague

We stand together
on the windy platform;
how sharp the rails
running out of sight
through the wet fields!

Carnew, the station master,
is peering over
his frosted window:
the hand of the signal
points down.

Crowned with churns
a cart creaks up
the incline of Main Street
to the sliding doors
of the Co-Op.

A smell of coal,
the train is coming...
You climb slowly in,
propped by my hand to
a seat, back to the engine,

and we leave, waving
a plume of black smoke
over the rushy meadows,
small hills and hidden villages —
Beragh, Carrickmore,

Pomeroy, Fintona —
place names that sigh
like a pressed melodeon
across this forgotten
Northern landscape.

A FLOWERING ABSENCE

How can one make an absence flower,
lure a desert to sudden bloom?
Taut with terror, I rehearse a time
when I was taken from a sick room:
as before from your flayed womb.

And given away to be fostered
wherever charity could afford.
I came back, lichened with sores,
from the care of still poorer
immigrants, new washed from the hold.

I bless their unrecorded names,
whose need was greater than mine,
wet nurses from tenement darkness
giving suck for a time
because their milk was plentiful

Or their own children gone.
They were the first to succour
that still terrible thirst of mine,
a thirst for love and knowledge,
to learn something of that time

Of confusion, poverty, absence.
Year by year I track it down
intent for a hint of evidence,
seeking to manage the pain —
how a mother gave away her son.

I took the subway to the hospital
in darkest Brooklyn, to call
on the old nun who nursed you
through the travail of my birth
to come on another cold trail.

'Sister Virgilius, how strange!
She died, just before you came.
She was delirious, rambling of all
her old patients; she could well
have remembered your mother's name.'

Around the bulk of St Catherine's
another wild, raunchier Brooklyn:
as tough a territory as I've known,
strutting young Puerto Rican hoods,
flash of blade, of bicycle chain.

Mother, my birth was the death
of your love life, the last man
to flutter near your tender womb:
a neon lit bar sign winks off & on,
motherfucka, thass your name.

There is an absence, real as presence.
In the mornings I hear my daughter
chuckle, with runs of sudden joy.
Hurt, she rushes to her mother,
as I never could, a puling boy.

All roads wind backwards to it.
An unwanted child, a primal hurt.
I caught fever on the big boat
that brought us away from America —
away from my lost parents.

Surely my father loved me,
teaching me to croon, *Ragtime Cowboy*
Joe, swaying in his saddle
as he sings, as he did, drunkenly
dropping in from the speakeasy.

So I found myself shipped back
to his home, in an older country,
transported to a previous century,
where his sisters restored me,
natural love flowering around me.

And the hurt ran briefly underground
to break out in a schoolroom
where I was taunted by a mistress
who hunted me publicly down
to near speechlessness.

'So this is our brightest infant?
Where did he get that outlandish accent?
What do you expect, with no parents,
sent back from some American slum:
none of you are to speak like him!'

Stammer, impediment, stutter:
she had found my lode of shame,
and soon I could no longer utter
those magical words I had begun
to love, to dolphin delight in.

And not for two stumbling decades
would I manage to speak straight again.
Grounded for the second time
my tongue became a rusted hinge
until the sweet oils of poetry

eased it and grace flooded in.

THE LOCKET

Sing a last song
for the lady who has gone,
fertile source of guilt and pain.
The worst birth in the annals of Brooklyn,
that was my cue to come on,
my first claim to fame.

Naturally she longed for a girl,
and all my infant curls of brown
couldn't excuse my double blunder
coming out, both the wrong sex,
and the wrong way around.
Not readily forgiven,

So you never nursed me
and when all my father's songs
couldn't sweeten the lack of money,
'when poverty comes through the door
love flies up the chimney',
your favourite saying,

Then you gave me away,
might never have known me,
if I had not cycled down
to court you like a young man,
teasingly untying your apron,
drinking by the fire, yarning

Of your wild, young days
which didn't last long, for you,
lovely Molly, the belle of your small town,
landed up mournful and chill
as the constant rain that lashes it
wound into your cocoon of pain.

Standing in that same hallway,
'Don't come again,' you say roughly,
'I start to get fond of you, John,
and then you are up and gone';
the harsh logic of a forlorn woman
resigned to being alone.

And still, mysterious blessing,
I never knew, until you were gone,
that always around your neck,
you wore an oval locket
with an old picture in it,
of a child in Brooklyn.

from

MOUNT EAGLE

(1989)

Semiotics

Loudest of all our protests when
the Deaf Mute Club of Ireland gather
to honour a brother, slammed down
by an abrupt bullet, near his Council home.
Challenged, he could only wave to answer
some tense and trigger-happy soldier.
Upon the broad British Embassy steps
the spokesman of the Deaf Mutes
makes an impassioned, fiery speech
in sign language. Fierce applause.
What officials spy through windows
of those comfortable Georgian rooms
is a flickering semaphore of fingers,
then an angry swirl of palms.

Cassandra's Answer

1.

All I can do is curse, complain.
I told you the flames would come
and the small towns blaze. Though

Precious little you did about it!
Obdurate. Roots are obstructions
as well as veins of growth.

How my thick tongue longs
for honey's ease, the warm
full syllables of praise

Instead of this gloomy procession
of casualties, clichés of decease;
deaf mutes' clamouring palms.

To have one subject only,
fatal darkness of prophecy,
gaunt features always veiled.

I have forgotten how I sang
as a young girl, before my voice
changed, and I tolled funerals.

I feel my mouth grow heavy again,
a storm cloud is sailing in;
a street will receive its viaticum

in the fierce release of a bomb.
Goodbye, Main Street, Fintona,
goodbye to the old Carney home.

2.

To step inside a childhood home,
tattered rafters that the dawn
leaks through, brings awareness

Bleaker than any you have known.
Whole albums of Births, Marriages,
roomfuls of tears and loving confidences

Gone as if the air has swallowed them;
stairs which climb towards nothing,
walls hosed down to flaking stone:

you were born inside a skeleton.

Turnhole

We part the leaves.

Small, squat, naked,
Jim Toorish stood in
the churning middle
of Clarkes' turnhole.

Black hair on his poll,
a roll of black hair
over his stomach, that
strange tussock below.

With a rib of black
fur along his back
from thick neckbone
to simian buttocks.

From which — *inescapable* —
his father root sprang,
gross as a truncheon,
normal as a pump-handle.

And cheerfully splashing,
scooping chill waters over
his curls, his shoulders —
that hairy thing!

To cleanse everything
but our prurient giggling
which took long years
for me to exorcise

Until I saw him again,
upright and glorious,
a satyr, laughing in
the spray at Florence.

Matins

That final bright morning you climb
The stairs to my balcony bed,
Unasked; unashamed: naked.
Barely a please was said
But in the widening light
Our bodies linked, blazed,
Our spirits melded. The dawn
Of a capital city swarmed
Beneath us, but we were absorbed,
Your long hair tenting your head,
Your body taut as a divining rod.
There is in such exchanges a harvest,
A source or wellspring of sweetness,
Grace beyond sense, body's intelligence.

Crossing

Your lithe and golden body
haunts me, as I haunt you:
corsairs with different freights
who may only cross by chance
    on lucky nights.

So our moorings differ.
But scents of your pleasure
still linger disturbingly
around me: fair winds or
    squalls of danger?

There is a way of forgetting you,
but I have forgotten it:
prepared wildly to cut free,
to lurch, like a young man,
    towards ecstasy!

Nightly your golden body turns
and turns in my shuddering dream.
Why is the heart never still,
yielding again to the cardinal
    lure of the beautiful?

Age should bring its wisdom
but in your fragrant presence
my truths are one, swirling
to a litany — sweet privateer —
    of grateful adulation.

Harvest

That first wild summer
we watched each other,
my greying hair and
wary eyes slowly drawn
to be warmed by your
flaring hair, abundant body.

No ice princess, you call
me down from my high tower —
on our first night together
I awoke, to watch over
your rich shape, a shower
of gold in the moonlight.

And an old fable stirred:
a stag rising from a wet brake —
Danae deluged by Zeus?
Rather, youth's promise fulfilled,
homely as a harvest field
from my Tyrone childhood

Where I hoist warm sheaves
to tent them into golden stooks,
each detail, as I wade
through the moonlit stubble,
crayon bright, as in
a child's colouring book.

Discords

1.

There is a white light in the room.
It is anger. He is angry, or
She is angry, or both are angry.
To them it is absolute, total,
It is everything; but to the visitor,
The onlooker, the outsider,
It is the usual, the absurd;
For if they did not love each other
Why should they heed a single word?

2.

Another sad goodbye at the airport;
Neither has much to say, *en garde*,
Lest a chance word turn barbed.
You bring me, collect me, each journey
Not winged as love, but heavy as duty;
Lohengrin's swan dipping to Charon's ferry.

3.

A last embrace at the door,
Your lovely face made ugly
By a sudden flush of tears
Which tell me more than any phrase,
Tell me what I most need to hear,
Wash away and cleanse my fears:
You have never ceased to love me.

She Cries

She puts her face against the wall
and cries, crying for herself,
crying for our children, crying
for all of us
                in this strange age
of shrinking space, with the needle
of Concorde saluting Mount Gabriel
with its supersonic boom, soaring
from London or Paris to Washington,
a slender, metallic, flying swan

and all the other paraphernalia, hidden
missiles hoarded in silos, bloated
astronauts striding the dusty moon,
and far beyond, our lonely message,
that long probe towards Venus,

but most of all for her husband
she cries, against the wall,
the poet at his wooden desk,
that toad with a jewel in his head,
no longer privileged, but still
trying to crash, without faltering,
the sound barrier, the dying word.

Sibyl's Morning

1.

She wakes in a hand-painted cot,
chats and chortles to herself,
a healthy small being, a happy elf,
sister to the early train whistle,
the bubbling dawn chorus along
the wisteria of Grattan Hill.

No complaints as yet, enjoying
through curtains the warm sunlight,
until she manages to upend herself.
Then the whine starts. Is it anger
or lust for the bottle?

Lift her up, warm and close
or held at arm's length—
that smell, like a sheep pen,
a country hedge steaming after rain.
As the bottle warms the decibels increase,

the scaldie's mouth gapes open;
head numb, coated tongue,
cortex ends squealing, no
thirsty drunk at a bar, nursing
a hangover, manages such concentration.

Daughter, dig in, with fists like ferns
unfurling, to basic happiness!
Little one, you are now
nothing but the long music of the gut,
a tug of life, with halts
for breathing, stomach swelling.

2.

On your throne afterwards
bang your heels, examine your new
and truly wonderful hands,
try out, warm up, your
little runs of satisfaction.

Day by day they also grow,
sound experiments in the laboratory
of the self, animal happiness,
the tonal colour of rage, cartoon
attempts to communicate, eyes beaming,
burbles rising. Best of all when

like any bird or beast waking,
you wail to yourself, with whoops,
finger stuffed gurgles, and my reward
for the morning, your speciality
(after the peristaltic hiccup)
when you smile and squeal with
sudden, sharp whistles —
O my human kettle!

Tea Ceremony

She brings us to her secret place, behind the apple tree, on the last
terrace of our garden. Ordering her little friends bossily, she leads
them first up the ladder; we follow behind, bashful giants. She has
set up a table, a few boards balanced on stones where a half-broken
doll sits facing a bruised teddy. One by one, large and small, we are
assigned our places: 'now *you* sit there' and '*you* sit here'. Then a fresh
batch of orders arrives. 'Since I'm the Mummy I pour out the tea.' A
child's hand reaches out, plucks and distributes china cups so delicate
that they are invisible. Then it grasps a teapot handle out of space and
leans across to each of us in turn, before settling back that solid object
made of air down in front of her. 'And here are the sandwiches and
biscuits.' Each of us receives a dusty twig or leaf. 'Now you all eat up
and if any of you complain I'll tell Daddy on you.' She gives Teddy an
affectionate poke which sends him sprawling to the ground. 'And sit
up straight: no slouching when we have visitors.' Solemnly we lift the
cups to our lips, toasting each other silently. Through the branches
of the apple tree we can see the city, a pall of smoke over the docks,
the opaque matte surface of the River Lee. Beyond those small hills
is the airport and as we drink invisibility a plane climbs, a sliver of
silver in the sunlight. Filtered through the apple blossom its sound
is as distant and friendly as the hum of a honey-seeking bee.

A Small Death

My daughter, Oonagh, wanders
off to play in the forest,
unafraid, her new rag doll
clutched under one arm:
a small fairy queen, trail-
ed by her elderly knight.

At the centre I find her
beneath black hemlock, red cedar,
halted on a carpet, a compost
of fallen leaves, rusty haws
and snowberries, knobbly chestnuts:
decay's autumnal weft.

She has found a dead bird
which she holds up in her
other hand; eyes, bright beads,
but the long beak spiky, cold,
twig legs crisped inwards.
Why not fly? she demands

And as I kneel to explain
(taking the retted corpse away)
dead, she repeats, puzzled.
So we bury the scant body
under a mound of damp leaves,
a gnome's pyre, a short barrow:

Her first funeral ceremony.
Home now, I nudge gently,
past the slapping branches,
the shallow Pacific rain pools
she loves ploutering through
in her diminutive wellingtons.

Beyond the tall woods lights
of Victoria are flickering on;
yellow flares of sodium
under dark coastal clouds
crossing Vancouver Island:
dream cattle swaying home.

Nest

When all the birds
    in the nest are there,
is that the start
    of a new despair?

The Black Lake

Across the black lake
Two figures row their boat
With slow, leaning strokes.
The grind of their rowlocks
Is rhythmic as a heartbeat.

Seven stooks stand
In a moonwashed field —
Seven pillars of gold —
While, beyond, two haystacks
Roped down to the earth.

Three lean cattle munch
The heavy aftergrass, or
Raise their heads towards
A stonewalled corner where
A couple lean from each other.

The moon climbs the hill.
The night brims with light,
A pantry, silent with milk.
The rowers reach the cottage,
The couple do not speak.

Luggala

for Garech Browne

Again and again in dream, I return to that shore. There is a wind
rising, a gull is trying to skim over the pines, and the waves whisper
and strike along the bright sickle of the little strand. Shoving through
reeds and rushes, leaping over a bog-brown stream, I approach the
temple by the water's edge, death's shrine, cornerstone of your sad-
ness. I stand inside, by one of the pillars of the mausoleum, and watch
the water in the stone basin. As the wind ruffles cease a calm surface
appears, like a mirror or crystal. And into it your face rises, sad beyond
speech, sad with an acceptance of blind, implacable process. For by
this grey temple are three tombs, a baby brother, a half-sister and a
grown brother, killed at twenty-one. Their monuments of Wicklow
granite are as natural here as the scattered rocks, but there is no prom-
ise of resurrection, only the ultimate silence of the place, the shale
littered face of the scree, the dark, dark waters of the glacial lake.

Mount Eagle

1.

The eagle looked at this changing world;
sighed and disappeared into the mountain.

Before he left he had a last reconnoitre:
the multi-coloured boats in the harbour

nodded their masts and a sandy white
crescent of strand smiled back at him.

How he liked the slight, drunk lurch
of the fishing fleet, the tide hoist-

ing them a little, at their ropes' end.
Beyond, wrack, and the jutting rocks

emerging, slowly, monsters stained
and slimed with strands of seaweed.

Ashore, beached boats and lobster-
pots, settled as hens in the sand.

2.

Content was life in its easiest form;
another was the sudden growling storm

which the brooding eagle preferred,
bending his huge wings into the winds'

wild buffeting, or thrusting down along
the wide sky, at an angle, slideways

to survey the boats, scurrying homewards,
tacking against the now contrary winds,

all of whom he knew by their names.
To be angry in the morning, calmed

by midday, but brooding again in
the evening was all in a day's quirk

with lengthy intervals for silence,
gliding along, like a blessing, while

the fleet toiled on earnestly beneath
him, bulging with a fine day's catch.

3.

But now he had to enter the mountain.
Why? Because a cliff had asked him?

The whole world was changing, with one
language dying, and another encroaching,

bright with buckets, cries of children.
There seemed to be no end to them,

and the region needed a guardian —
so the mountain had told him. And

a different destiny lay before him:
to be the spirit of that mountain.

Everyone would stand in awe of him.
When he was wrapped in the mist's caul

they would withdraw because of him,
peer from behind blind or curtain.

When he lifted his wide forehead
bold with light, in the morning,

they would all laugh and smile with him.
It was a greater task than an eagle's

aloofness, but sometimes, under his oilskin
of coiled mist, he sighs for lost freedom.

The Hill of Silence

1.

From the platform
of large raised stones

lines appear to lead us
along the hillside

bog tufts softening
beneath each step

bracken and briar
restraining our march

clawing us back, slowing
us to perception's pace.

2.

A small animal halts,
starts, leaps away

and a lark begins
its dizzy, singing climb

towards the upper skies
and now another stone appears

ancient, looming, mossed,
long ago placed,

lifted to be a signpost
along the old path.

3.

Let us climb further.
As one thought leads
to another, so one lich-

ened snout of stone
still leads one on,
beckons to a final one.

4.

Under its raised slab
thin trickles of water

gather to a shallow pool
in which the headstone

mirrors, and rears
to regard its shadow self,

and a diligent spider weaves
a trembling, silver web,

a skein of terrible delicacy
swaying to the wind's touch,

a fragile, silken scarf,
a veined translucent leaf.

5.

This is the slope of loneliness.
This is the hill of silence.
This is the wind's fortress.
Our world's polestar.
A stony patience.

6.

We have reached a shelf
that surveys the valley

on these plains below
a battle flowed and ebbed

and the gored, spent warrior
was ferried up here

where water and herbs
might staunch his wounds.

7.

Let us also lay ourselves
down in this silence

let us also be healed
wounds closed, senses cleansed

as over our bowed heads
the mad larks multiply

needles stabbing the sky
in an ecstasy of stitching fury

against the blue void
while from clump and tuft

cranny and cleft, soft-footed
curious, the animals gather around.

from

TIME IN ARMAGH

(1993)

6. Time in Armagh

I, too, drew my hand back from the cane.
                                    —Juvenal

1.

Hazing, they call it in America,
but I already knew it from Armagh,
the fledgeling hauled to the pump,

protesting, by the bigger boys
to be baptised with his nickname,
Froggy, Screwy, Rubberneck or *Dopey,*

some shameful blemish, his least attract-
ive aspect, hauled out to harry, haunt him
through his snail years in St Patrick's,

a five-year sentence. Even in the chapel,
in that hush of prayers and incense
the same cruelty was ritually practised,

shoving the prongs of the dividers
into the thighs of the smaller boy
who knelt before you. He couldn't cry

in such a sacred atmosphere, disturb
the priest murmuring on the altar,
the tinkle for the lofted Eucharist.

Sometimes they used a Sacred Heart pin
to jab the victim. Tears spilt down
his face, while the Blessed Virgin

smiled inside the altar rails, and
Christ stumbled from station to station
around our walls, to His crucifixion,

thorn-spiked, our exemplary victim.

2.

Then there was the gym and Gaelic football,
both compulsory. Dopey hid down a manhole
to escape these Spartan training sessions

where his slower wits betrayed him
to more jibes and taunts. He held on
but thirty years later, a grown man,

he began to break down, a boy, weeping,
plunged in the pit again, long hours waiting
in that damp darkness, until he heard

the thud of studded boots above his head.

3.

Endless games designed to keep us pure—
'Keep your hands out of your pockets, boys'—
we wore togs even in the showers.

No wonder Donaghy fired a brick through
a window when he left. 'I loathed every hour,
every minute,' wrote Des from Bangor,

'what you learnt was to be a survivor.
Remember our eccentric English music master;
what you need is a jolly good six-ah!'

Which, gentle soul, he never administered.
But those of the order of Melchisedech
were no slouches when it came to the stick.

Father Roughan, all too rightly named,
had a fine selection of swishing canes,
test-lashing the air before he landed one

right down the middle of the open palm,
or tingling along the shaking fingertips,
until the hand was ridged with welts.

Dismissed, the boys tried to hide
and hug their hurt under the armpits,
not a whimper, until safely outside

where the cub pack huddled around them,
offering the cold comfort of admiration:
sudden conspiracy of bully and victim

united before the black-skirted enemy.
Our stiff upper lip was an Ulster clamp.
No whingeing. No quarter for the crybaby.

Still to this late day I rage blind
whenever I hear that hectoring tone,
trying to put another human being down.

The guilt givers who know what is right,
they can shove their rules. A system
without love is a crock of shite.

7. Waiting

Halting in Dungannon between trains
We often wandered outside town
To see the camp where German
Prisoners were kept. A moist litter
Of woodshavings showed
Ground hastily cleared, and then—

The huge parallelogram
Of barbed wire, nakedly measured
And enclosed like a football field
With the guard towers rising, aloof
As goalposts, at either end.

Given length and breadth we knew
The surface area the prisoners paced
As one hung socks to dry outside
His Nissen hut, another tried
To hum and whistle 'Lili Marlene':
They seemed to us much the same

As other adults, except in their
Neutral dress, and finding it normal
To suffer our gaze, like animals,
As we squatted and pried, for an hour
Or more, about their human zoo

Before it was time for shopfronts,
Chugging train, Vincentian school.
A small incident, soon submerged
In our own brisk, bell-dominated rule:
Until, years later, I saw another camp—
Rudshofen, in the fragrant Vosges—

Similar, but with local improvements:
The stockade where they knelt the difficult,
The laboratory for minor experiments,
The crematorium for Jews and gypsies
Under four elegant pine towers, like minarets.

This low-pitched style seeks exactness,
Determined not to betray the event.
But as I write the grid of barbed
Wire rises abruptly around me,
The smell of woodshavings plugs
My nostrils, a carrion stench.

9. History Walk

Our History Master was a curly-headed young priest who leaned too close to us in class, the better to inspect our copybooks, *moryah*. Often I felt his downy cheek press against mine, though I doubt if he knew what he was doing: he was as ignorant and naive as the rest of us. Yet he could wax enthusiastic; in our first term, before the official NI Syllabus swallowed us, we learnt about something called Early Irish Civilisation. I loved it, Larne flints, osiered banquet halls, the bronze trumpet of Lough na Shade. *Then it was back to the Origins of the Industrial Revolution.*

Once myth and reality warmly met, when we swarmed over Navan Fort. Sheep grazed where Cúchulainn and his High King, Conor, argued, a quarry ate the grass where Deirdre first saw her young warrior. But we were doing English and Modern History for our State exams, not Irish, so the mythic figures melted into the mizzling rain, the short views returned: we were standing on a large green hillock in the County Armagh, Northern Ireland, not on the magic mound of Emain Macha, the hillfort of the Red Branch knights. *There would surely be a question on William Pitt, and the Corn Laws.*

History Walks were rarer than Geography, perhaps because they feared to disturb our local nest of pismires. History lay about us in our infancy, with many levels, but only one stratum open. They did not have to explain to us why our new Cathedral had been built on a higher hill. We explored our ancient rival when we ran footloose through town. We marvelled at its echoing emptiness, the rotting flags of Imperial wars. The roll call in the side chapel of the Royal Irish Fusiliers might have taught us something: O's and Macs mingled in death with good Proddy names, Hamilton, Hewitt, Taylor, Acheson.

Instead we ran down the curling, cobbled hill, giggling with guilt. Doomed as any Armada, the lost city of Ard Macha coiled in upon itself, whorl upon whorl, a broken aconite. Layer upon layer had gone to its making, from Cúchulainn to St Patrick, from fleet-footed Macha to Primate Robinson's gaggle of Georgian architects. But the elegance of the Mall was of no avail against simpleminded sectarianism; Armagh, a maimed capital, a damaged pearl.

We sensed this as we sifted through the shards in the little County Museum. Bustled around the glass cases by Curly Top, we halted before a Yeoman's coat, alerted by our party song, 'The Croppy Boy'. And we read about the battle of Diamond Hill between 'Peep-o'-Day Boys' and Catholic Defenders which led to the founding of the Orange Order at Loughgall, a canker among the apple blossoms.

We did not discuss this in our History Class which now dealt with the origins of the First World War, from the shot in Sarajevo. It did crop up in RK, Religious Knowledge, where the Dean warned us against the dangers of Freemasonry. A Catholic could never become King of England or President of the United States; everywhere the black face of Protestantism barred the way to good Catholic boys. Amongst the cannon on the Mall the Protestant boys played cricket, or kicked a queer shaped ball like a pear. According to my Falls Road pal Protestant balls bounced crooked as the Protestants themselves. One day that banter would stop when a shot rang out on the Cathedral Road.

10. Absence

One by one the small boys nod off.
The only light left, my Prefect's torch.
For an hour I have patrolled the dorm,
Checking that Romeo Forte is not snoring,
That Gubby Lenny is not homesick, weeping,
The terrible O'Neill twins not whispering.
Surely Dean Roughan will not do the rounds
Tonight, so I have a chance to warm up again
My letter to a convent girl in Lurgan,
Concealed inside my Modern History volume.
I can still smell the fragrance of your hair,
Your small ears, like seashells, and so on.
The water pipes knock, the great bells sound.
To the chill dark of my cubicle I summon
The sweet blessing of a girlish presence,
Shaping my lips to kiss her absence.

13. Stone

Cathedral,
I shape you in the air with my hands,
On a night when a cutting wind
Counts the hours
With chill bursts of rain.

Cathedral,
Tall-spired guardian of my childhood
In the Ulster night,
Over Saint Patrick's city
The rooves are eyelashed with rain

As the iron bell
Swings out again, each quarter's notes
Dwindling down a shaft of past
And present, to drown
In that throat of stone.

I lived in Armagh in a time of war,
The least conscious time of my life.
Between two stones may lie
My future self
Waiting that you pass by.

If she pass by,
Dislodging the stone of my youth,
Cathedral,
Enclosure and cloister, prow of lost surety,
Resound for me!

BORDER SICK CALL

(1995)

for Seamus Montague, MD, my brother, in memory of a journey
in winter along the Fermanagh-Donegal border.

Looks like I'm breakin' the ice!

— *Fats Waller*

Weary, God!
of starfall and snowfall,
weary of north winter, and weary
of myself like this, so cold and thoughtful.

— *Hayden Carruth*

1.

Hereabouts signs are obliterated,
but habit holds.

We wave a friendly goodbye
to a Customs Post that has twice
leaped into the air
to come to earth again
as a makeshift, a battered trailer
hastily daubed green: *An Stad.*

The personnel still smile
and wave back,
their limbs still intact.

Fragments of reinforced concrete,
of zinc, timber, sag and glint in the hedge
above them, the roof and walls
of their old working place:

> *Long years in France,*
> *I have seen little like this,*
> *même dans la guerre algérienne,*
> *the impossible as normal,*
> *lunacy made local,*
> *surrealism made risk.*

Along the glistening main road
snowplough-scraped, salt-sprinkled,
we sail, chains clanking,
the surface bright, hard, treacherous,
with only one slow, sideways skid
before we reach the side road.

Along ruts ridged with ice
the car now rocks until we reach
a gap walled with snow where
silent folk wait and watch
for our, for your, arrival.

The high body of a tractor
rides us a few extra yards
on its caterpillar wheels
till it also slips and slopes
into a hidden ditch
to tilt helpless, one large
welted tyre spinning.

2.

Shanks' mare now, it seems,
for the middle-aged,
marching between hedges
burdened with snow,
low bending branches
which sigh to the ground
as we pass, to spring back.

And the figures fall back
with soft murmurs of
'on the way home, doctor?'
shades that disappear
to merge into the fields,
their separate holdings.

Only you seem to know
where you are going
as we march side by side,

following the hillslope
whose small crest shines
like a pillar of salt,
only the so solid scrunch
and creak of snow crystals
thick-packed underneath
your fur boots, my high
farmer's wellingtons.

Briefly we follow
the chuckling rush
of a well-fed stream
that swallows, and swells
with the still-melting snow
until it loses itself
in a lough, a mountain tarn
filmed with crisp ice
which now flashes sunlight,
a mirror of brightness,
reflecting, refracting
a memory, a mystery:

> *Misty afternoons in winter*
> *we climb to a bog pool;*
> *rushes fossilized in ice.*
> *A run up, and a slide —*
> *boots score a glittering*
> *path, until a heel slips*
> *and a body measures its length*
> *slowly on ice, starred with*
> *cracks like an old plate.*

Into this wide, white world
we climb slowly higher,
no tree or standing stone,

only cold sun and moorland,
where a stray animal,
huddled, is a dramatic event,
a gate a silvered statement,
its bars burred with frost,
tracks to a drinking trough,
rutted hard as cement:
a silent, islanded cottage,
its thatch slumped in,
windows cracked, through which,
instead of Christians, cattle
peer out, in dumb desolation.

> And I remember how, in Fintona,
> you devoured Dante by the fireside,
> a small black World's Classic.
> But no purgatorial journey
> reads stranger than this,
> our Ulster border pilgrimage
> where demarcations disappear,
> landmarks, forms, and farms vanish
> into the ultimate coldness of an ice age,
> as we march towards Lettercran,
> in steel-blue, shadowless light,
> The Ridge of the Tree, the heart of whiteness.

3.

We might be astronauts creak-
ing over the cold curve
of the moon's surface, as our boots
sink, rasp over crusted snow,
sluggish, thick, dreamlike,

until, for the first time
in half-an-hour, we see
a human figure, shrunken
but agile, an old, old man
bending over something, poking
at it furiously with a stick:
carcass of fox or badger?

'Hello,' we hallo, like strangers
on an Antarctic or arctic ice floe—
Amundsen greeting a penguin! —
each detail in cold relief.

Hearing us, the small figure halts,
turns an unbelieving face, then
takes off, like a rabbit or hare
with a wounded leg, the stick its pivot,
as it hirples along, vigorously
in the wrong, the opposite
direction, away from us,
the stricken gait of the aged
transformed into a hobble,
intent as a lamplighter.

We watch as our pathfinder,
our potential guide, dwindles
down the valley, steadily
diminishing until
he burrows,
bolts under,
disappears into,
a grove of trees.

'And who might that be,
would you say?' I ask my brother
as we plod after him
at half his pace. 'Surely
one of my most urgent patients,'
he says, with a wry smile,
'the sick husband gone to get
his sicker wife back to bed
before I arrive.' And he smiles
again, resignedly.

'And, besides, he wants to tidy
the place up before the Doctor
comes. Things will be grand
when we finally get there:
he just wasn't expecting anyone
to brave the storm.

'But there'll be a good welcome
when we come.'

And sure enough all is waiting,
shining, inside the small cottage.
The fire laughs on the hearth,
bellows flared, whilst the dog rises
to growl, slink, then wag its tail.

4.

My brother is led into the bedroom.
Then himself, a large-eared, blue-eyed gnome,
still pert with the weight of his eighty years,
discourses with me before his hearth,
considerately, like a true host.

'Border, did you say,
how many miles to the border?
Sure we don't know where it starts
or ends up here, except we're lost
unless the doctor or postman finds us.

'But we didn't always complain.
Great hills for smuggling they were;
I made a packet in the old days,
when the big wars were rumbling on,
before this auld religious thing came in.

'You could run a whole herd through
between night and morning, and no one
the wiser, bar the B-Specials,
and we knew every mother's son
well enough to grease the palm,
quietlike, if you know what I mean.
Border be damned, it was a godsend.
Have you ever noticed, cows have no religion?'

　　Surefooted, in darkness,
　　stick-guiding his animals,
　　in defiance of human frontiers,
　　the oldest of Irish traditions,
　　the creach or cattle raid,
　　as ancient as the Táin.

Now, delighted with an audience,
my host rambles warmly on;
holding forth on his own hearth:

'Time was, there'd be a drop
of the good stuff in the house,'
the head cocked sideways

before he chances a smile,
'but not all is gone.
Put your hand in the thatch
there, left of the door,
and see what you find.'

Snug as an egg under a hen,
a small prescription bottle of colourless poteen.
'Take that medicine with you for the road home.
You were brave men to come.'

5.

Downhill, indeed, is easier,
while there is still strong light,
an eerie late afternoon glow
boosted by the sullen weight
of snow on the hedges,
still or bowing to the ground
again, as we pass, an ice-blue
whiteness beneath our steady tread;
a snow flurry, brief, diamond-hard,
under a frieze of horsetail cloud.

The same details of field, farm
unravelling once again, as the doctor
plods on, incongruous in his fur boots
(but goodness often looks out of place),
downhill, with the same persistence
in a setting as desolate as if
a glacier had just pushed off:

　　Thick and vertical
　　the glacier slowly

a green white wall
grinding mountains
scooping hollows
a gross carapace
sliding down the
face of Europe
to seep, to sink
its melting weight
into chilly seas;
bequeathing us
ridges of stone,
rubble of gravel,
eskers of hardness:
always within us —
a memory of coldness.

Only one detail glints different.
On that lough — where the sun burns
above the silver ice, like a calcined stone,
a chilling fire, orange red —
a row boat rests, chained in ice,
ice at gunwhale, prow and stern,
ice jagged on the anchor ropes;
still, frozen, 'the small bark of my wit',
la navicella del mio ingegno.
Why could I not see it on the way
up, only on the journey home,

I wonder, as my brother briefly disappears
across the half-door of another house,
leaving me to wait, as glimmers gather
into the metallic blues of twilight,
and watch (as if an inward eye were opening)
details expand in stereoscopic brightness;
a buck hare, not trembling, unabashed,

before he bounds through the frozen grass,
a quick scatter of rabbits, while
a crow clatters to the lower wood,
above the incessant cries of the sheep herd.

6.

When my brother returns, breath pluming,
although he risks only a swallow,
the fiery drink unleashes his tongue:
from taciturn to near-vision,

'I heard you chatting to old MacGurren,
but the real border is not between
countries, but between life and death,
that's where the doctor comes in.

'I have sat beside old and young
on their deathbeds, and have seen
the whole house waiting, as for birth,
everything scoured, spick-and-span,
footsteps tiptoeing around.

'But the pain is endless,
you'd think no one could endure it,
but still they resist, taste the respite,
until the rack tightens again
on the soiled, exhausted victim.'

> But the poem is endless,
> the poem is strong as our weakness,
> strong in its weakness,
> it will never cease until it has said
> what cannot be said.

The sighs and crying of someone
who is leaving this world
in all its solid, homely detail
for another they have only heard tell of,
in the hearsay called religion,
or glimpsed uneasily in dream.

'People don't speak of it,
lacking a language for this terrible thing,
a forbidden subject, a daily happening,
pushed aside until it comes in.
I remember the first time I saw it
on my first post as a locum.'

(That smell in the sickroom —
stale urine and faeces —
the old man on the grey bed,
his wife crouched in darkness.

Many generations of family
lined up along the stairs
and out into the farmyard:
the youngest barely aware

of the drama happening inside
that unblinking frame of light;
but horseplaying, out loud.
Three generations, and the tree shaking.

He has lain still for months
but now his muscles tighten,
he lifts himself into a last
bout of prayers and imprecations.

The old woman also starts up
but there is no recognition,
only that ultimate effort, before
he falls back, broken,

The rosary lacing stiff fingers.)
'I did not expect to witness
the process in such a rush:
it still happens in these lost places.'

7.

Just as we think we are finally clear
another shade steps out from the shadows
(out of the darkness, they gather to your goodness),
with its ritual murmured demand:
'Doctor, would you be so good to come in?
The wife is taken bad again.'

All the clichés of rural comedy
(which might be a rural tragedy)
as he leads us along a tangled path,
our clabbery *via smaritta*.

Briars tug at us, thorn and whin
jag us, we trudge along a squelching drain;
my brother and I land ankle-deep in slush,
a gap guttery as a boghole,
and he has to haul us out by hand,
abjectly, 'Sorry we've no back lane.'

In his house, where an Aladdin burns,
we step out of our boots, socks,

before the warm bulk of the Rayburn,
and my brother pads, barefooted,
into the back room, where a woman moans.

Nursing a mug of tea in the kitchen
I confer anxiously with her cowed man.
'She's never been right since the last wain,
God knows, it's hard on the women.'

Three ragged little ones in wellingtons
stare at the man from Mars,
suck their thumbs and say nothing.
There is a tinny radio but no television.
A slight steam rises where our socks hang.
At last my brother beckons him in.

When we leave, no more conversation;
the labourer stumbling before us,
his hand shielding a candle
which throws a guttering flame:
a sheltering darkness of firs, then,
spiked with icicles, a leafless thorn,
where the gate scringes on its stone.

When we stride again on the road,
there is a bright crop of stars,
the high, clear stars of winter,
the studded belt of Orion,
and a silent, frost-bright moon
upon snow crisp as linen
spread on death-or-bridal bed;
blue tinged as a spill of new
milk from the crock's lip.

8.

Another mile, our journey is done.
The main road again. The snow-laden car
gleams strange as a space machine.

We thrust snow from the roof;
sit cocooned as the engine warms,
and the wipers work their crescents clean

with a beat steady as a metronome.
Brother, how little we know of each other!
Driving from one slaughter to another

once, you turned on the car radio
to hear the gorgeous pounding rhythms
of your first symphony: Beethoven.

In the face of suffering, unexpected affirmation.
For hours we've been adrift from humankind,
navigating our bark in a white landlocked ocean.

Will a stubborn devotion suffice,
sustained by an ideal of service?
Will dogged goodwill solve anything?

Headlights carve a path through darkness
back through Pettigo, towards Enniskillen.
The customs officials wave us past again.

But in what country have we been?

from

SMASHING THE PIANO

(1999)

Paths

We had two gardens.

A real flower garden
overhanging the road
(our miniature Babylon).
Paths which I helped
to lay with Aunt Winifred
riprapped with pebbles;
shards of painted delph;
an old potato boiler;
a blackened metal pot
now bright with petals.

Hedges of laurel, palm.
A hovering scent of boxwood.
Crouched in the flowering
lilac, I could oversee
the main road, old Lynch
march to the well-spring
with his bucket, whistling,
his carroty sons herding
in and out their milch cows;
a growing whine of cars.

Then, the vegetable garden
behind, rows of broad beans
plumping their cushions,
the furled freshness of
tight little lettuce heads,
slim green pea-pods above
early flowering potatoes,
gross clumps of carrots,
parsnips, a frailty of parsley,
a cool fragrance of mint.

Sealed off by sweetpea
clambering up its wired fence,
the goats' tarred shack
which stank in summer,
in its fallow, stone-heaped corner.

With, on the grassy margin,
a well-wired chicken run,
cheeping balls of fluff
brought one by one into the sun
from their metallic mother —
the paraffin incubator —
always in danger from
the marauding cat, or
the stealthy, hungry vixen:
I their small guardian.

Two gardens, the front
for beauty, the back
for use. Sleepless now
I wander through both
and it is summer again,
the long summers of youth,
as I trace small paths
in a trance of growth:
flowers pluck at my coat
as I bend down to help
or speak to my aunt
whose calloused hands
caressing the plants
are tender as a girl's.

Still Life, with Aunt Brigid

Still nourished by her care
and love which never seems to fail,
not only through ceaseless prayer,
but like an attendant angel
sensed, a hovering fragrance
against the plainest of backgrounds;
as, crossing the cobbles at night
on some last errand (are the hens
locked in safely, the calves foddered,
the yard gate looped closed?)
the swaying light of the storm lamp
or a hand-sheltered candle, flickers
around her frail figure, limned in gold
and shadows, like a Rembrandt.

FROM Kindertotenlieder

1. TIME OFF

A bleaching sun on Rarogan Hill;
lifting the falling corn, plaiting the sheaves,
a man's work, but Martha bustles to please,
more at ease than in the schoolroom
where so often she extends an open palm.

The cattle suck the salt lick,
huddle under the trees, or break
clumsily wild while the triangle
of stubborn corn shrinks steadily before
the machine's shuddering teeth.

On the second day she wilts,
complains of a brow bound in pain,
a heat blur before her eyes.
She is told to work on and,
when she fumbles, gruffly criticised.

The sun burns; the rain holds off.
The men are too intent to return
to the house for a cool drink, or aspirin.
The reaper is hired and, as it rattles
and races to bite the stalks,

the sheaves are still to bind.
At twilight Martha slumps like a grain sack.
They trudge her heavy body home.
For three days they cannot return.
Even a child's funeral takes time.

Between

for Michael Viney

That deep, dark pool. To come upon it,
after driving across the Gap in midsummer,
the hedges freighted with fuchsia, hawthorn,
blood-red and white under shining veils of rain.

A wind flurry finecombing the growing grain
as a full-uddered cow precedes us along the lane,
a curious calf poking its lubberly head over stone
while the country road winds betwixt and between.

Sudden, at the summit of the Knockmealdowns,
a chill black lake, a glacial corrie or tarn,
some large absence, hacked, torn
from the far side of the dreaming cliff.

A brooding silence, a hoarded font of nothing,
lightless, still, opaque ... severely alone.
Except when a shiver, a skirl of wind,
makes the waters tremble, mild as that field of grain.

But on the shorn flank of the mountain
a flowering, flaring bank of rhododendron,
exalted as some pagan wedding procession.
Fathomless darkness, silent raging colour:

A contrast to make your secret self tremor,
like a child cradled in this quarry's murmur,
delighted but lost between the dark, the blossoming.
On one side, a moorland's bareness, rufous heather

sheltering a long-nebbed curlew, bog asphodel or lobelia
and, on the other, that terraced orchestra of colour,
avenues of lavish amethyst blossom.
Chill of winter: full warmth of summer,

colliding head on in stillness, and a heavy aroma.

The Current

I saunter down to Sarah Bailey's empty house;
some spinster, enshrined in local history
for living, solitary as a heron, or some

other bogpool-haunting creature
in this dank, small-windowed, loosely
mortared stone nest by the ceaseless rush
of the Garvaghey river...

                Walls piled
with straw, it provides winter shelter
for cattle who bruise their warm backs
against each other, as I enter stealthily,
my feet crackling on the strewn fodder,
or sinking into fetlocked depths of dung, mud,
of what was once her clay floor. Other boys
and I met here to share sticky sweets
and cigarettes (a cache behind a loose stone),
plotting devilment, away from home,
away from parents. And it was nearby
I first learnt a mystery, as everyone must,
striking matches against the encroaching dark.

An older boy leads me aside, crawling
down a tunnel of dragging brambles,
a thicket of thorn, and bruise-coloured sloes,
to a dense ledge overlooking our river
where bog-brown water pours endlessly over
a waterfall's lip, whirling into frothy spittle.
We lie down on a pelt of emerald moss,
littered with twigs, resinous bark, speckled insects,
already rusting fronds of fern, sorrel,
watercress, clover.

              I trust him:
we have carried water from the same spring,
worked on the high bog. I watch
as he fumbles one by one the large metal buttons

of his dungarees, to uncover
a grotesque object, his much bigger cock,
its hammer head swollen with blood,
from which he draws the sheath back,
to show the raw flesh, nakeder than naked,
already glistening with threads of liquid.

A sight familiar from any jakes wall
but awesome to me as he wrinkles it
back and forward with an urging hand,
working the membrane of the foreskin,
a blue vein beating along the length of it,
from the tender, tightening bag of the balls
to that small moist eye, the slit

                              which gapes
like a gill, as he groans, gropes, and sighs.
Then his face stiffens as though in pain,
his body goes rigid. Something new happens,
something I have never dreamt or seen.
He shivers full length, and spills, shudders
some unknown white substance on the soft grass,
and I *must* watch as eerie, carnal-smelling sperm
drenches, mingles its warm, strange odour
of straw and loam with the wildflowers
across our hiding place.

                              (After a while,
we will talk of girls, courting, future loves?
He will fold away his now-shrunken cock,
or I will dare display my still slender effort
which I rub a little, without much effect.
Surely not the worst way to approach
love's central act, through friendship?)

But now he lies exhausted, spent,
as a gasping fish on the river bank.
We do not touch, rest quiet,
but, between us, over the moss,
shine the snail tracks of a secret
with, in the background, the hidden,

overheard pull and swirl of the current.

FROM Dark Rooms

1. WRATH

Lying in the darkness, grim with anger

against the one lying by your side,
herself, grim with anger
at your lying
so grim with anger by her side.

This night only absence will be her lover,
only wrath will be your bride.

There Are Days

There are days when
one should be able
to pluck off one's head
like a dented or worn
helmet, straight from
the nape and collarbone
(those crackling branches!)

and place it firmly down
in the bed of a flowing stream.
Clear, clean, chill currents
coursing and spuming through
the sour and stale compartments
of the brain, dimmed eardrums,
bleared eyesockets, filmed tongue.

And then set it back again
on the base of the shoulders:
well tamped down, of course,
the laved skin and mouth,
the marble of the eyes
rinsed and ready
for love; for prophecy?

FROM *Flower, Stone, Sea*

1. THE SMELL OF THE EARTH

   after Guillevic

At Carnac, the smell of the earth
has something not recognizable.

It is an odour of earth
perhaps, but transferred
to the level of geometry.

Where the wind, the sun, the salt,
the iodine, the bones, the sweet water of streams,
the dead seashells, the grasses, the slurry,
the saxifrage, the warmed stone, the bilge,
the still-wet linen, the tar of boats,
the byres, the whitewashed walls, the fig trees,

the old clothes of the people, their speech,
and always the wind, the sun, the salt,
the slightly disgusting loam, the dried seaweed,

all together and separately struggle
with the epoch of the menhirs

to measure up.

The Family Piano

My cousin is smashing the piano.
He is standing over its entrails
swinging a hatchet in one hand
and a hammer handle in the other
like a plundering Viking warrior.

My cousin is smashing the piano
and a jumble, jangle of eighty-eight keys
and chords, of sharps and flats
clambers to clutch at the hatchet,
recoils, to strike at his knees

(*My cousin is smashing the piano!*)
like the imploring hands of refugees
or doomed passengers on the Titanic
singing 'Nearer My God to Thee'
as they vanish into lit, voiceless seas.

My cousin is smashing the piano
Grandfather installed in the parlour
to hoop his children together.
It came in a brake from Omagh,
but now lists, splintered and riven.

My cousin is smashing the piano
where they gathered to sing in chorus
'My Bonny Lies Over the Ocean'
beneath the fading family portraits
of Melbourne Tom, Brooklyn John.

My cousin is smashing the piano
where buxom Aunt Winifred played
old tunes from scrolled songbooks,
serenely pressing the pedals and singing
'Little Brown Jug', 'One Man Went to Mow',

or (My cousin is smashing the piano)
hammered out a jig, 'The Irish Washerwoman',
while our collie dog lifted its long nose
and howled to high heaven:
John Cage serenading Stockhausen!

FROM Civil Wars

7. A RESPONSE TO OMAGH

All I can do is curse, complain.
Who can endorse such violent men
as history creaks on its bloody hinge
and the unspeakable is done again?

With no peace after the deluge,
no ease after the storm;
we learn to live inside ruin
like a second home.

Landing

for Elizabeth

They sparkle beneath our wings;
spilt jewel caskets, lights strewn
in rich darkness, lampstrings of pearls.

And then the plane tilts, a warm
intimate thrumming, like travelling within
the ambergris-heavy belly of a whale.

The abstract beauty of our world;
gleams anvilled to a glowing grid,
how the floor of earth is thick inlaid!

Traffic borne, lotus on a stream,
planes lofting, hovering, descending,
kites without strings, as I race homewards

towards you, beside whom I now belong,
age iam, meorum finis amorum,
my late, but final anchoring.

from

DRUNKEN SAILOR

(2004)

White Water

The light, tarred skin
of the currach rides
and receives the current,
rolls and responds to
the harsh sea swell.

Inside the wooden ribs
a slithering frenzy; a sheen
of black-barred silver-
green and flailing mackerel:
the iridescent hoop
of a gasping sea trout.

As a fish gleams most
fiercely before it dies,
so the scales of the sea-hag
shine with a hectic
putrescent glitter:

luminous, bleached —
white water —
that light in the narrows
before a storm breaks.

The Hag's Cove

Over the steeped, heaped seaweed
the flies, shimmering blue-black
and gold, sing their song of harvesting,
of dissolution, the necessary process
of putrefaction, decay's deadly drone.

Thick dragons' tails of wrack,
frilled flutter of dulse,
a song of things breaking down,
other things feeding upon them,
a compost heap of dissolving forms,
a psalm, a threnody of decomposition.

*

I made my way there, daily,
a sort of dark pilgrimage,
mind and body freshening
after the habitual soilings
(tensions of work, family,
ceaseless sour quarrels),
soothed by the ocean's
eternal turning flange,
its vast devouring indifference,
blue and calm, or bruised and folding
with angry, heaving motion.

*

Along the promontory
stand three stone towers,
not only 'dead at the top'
but hollowed, useless, except
as a sanctuary for wild animals,
for nestling birds, or lovers
fleeing the constant coastal rains.

Such a long time since compass,
spyglass and binoculars
watched and waited for
the great Atlantic liners,

Cunard and White Star,
carrying their cargo of pain away
(torn families, old-fashioned exile tears)
or, laden with success, returning
(the glossy suit of the prodigal son):
looming shapes at the mouth
of Cork's verdant, unfurling harbour.

*

One smashed down here, below,
a Captain drunk in his bunk
as his charge rammed the rocks;
caught and tossed all day
between the Cow and the Calf,
slowly smashed into smithereens;
now a hushed pub legend.

*

To allow oneself to be swallowed again,
repossessed by nature's thick sweetness
(Over the steeped, heaped seaweed
the flies sing their song of harvesting),
that hectic glitter of decay,
that gluttonous moil of creation,
to be smashed on the rocks,
broken down and built again,
clutching at the intimate softness
of tough reed, brave flower,
swaying at the cliff's edge,
like the mind on its fraying tether;
what shall we do with this drunken sailor
early in the morning?

Hermit

The night structures swarm-
ing around this attic room;
a silver trellis of stars,
tide wash, then silence.

Stir and creak of the fire,
an ikon bright on the wall
and, of course, books, papers,
hosts of silent dialogue.

To work intently while
the constellations shift
across the frost-sharp sky,
moisture condenses on the glass,

autumn yielding to winter,
Pegasus to the Hunter,
one year into another,
endless death, ceaseless birth,

while ships toil up the channel,
patient as the night prowl
of the owl, or probing heron;
the snail progress of a poem.

Intellect and universe
held briefly in tune,
under the blanched helm
of the cliff lighthouse,

upright and defiant
against the night,
a restless arm of light
shearing the dark.

Letter Valley

1. MARY KATE'S KITCHEN

The gate scringes upon its hollowed stone.

I feel I have stumbled back into my own:
old men brooding before a metal hearth,
women bustling between pantry and oilcloth,
a moon-faced wall clock and display of delph,
the girlish gravitas of the Virgin on her shelf.

A long way round to curve near home again,
kindling embers of a long-smoored self.

2. SCRIBE IN THE WOODS

after the Irish, 9th century

The birds sing on summer evenings.
A cheeky robin balances on the buoyant bough
of its favourite lichened tree outside my window,
whistling away, while here comes
a ragged convoy of crows
with their clatter, their funereal flapping home
to the higher branches.

After so many years I cannot translate
a word they are saying, signals they're exchanging.
Long conferences on telephone wires:
twittered alarms, melodious monotony,
notes arrayed along a staff,
while human messages course ceaselessly
beneath their taut claws.

The fuschia hedge trembles.
All those small
scarlet petals are shivering:
a mass of bells silently pealing
where the honeybees are clambering
like uniformed schoolboys swarming
up the slope to Armagh Cathedral,
or striped players ceaselessly scoring
inside those green and scarlet meshes
while the whole hedge trembles.

Head or Harp

The butt is a flat round stone.
The marker, a stroke in the dust.
Toecap to the line, sly ones thrust
their upper bodies forward, heron-tilted,
as the *pingin*, or penny, sails aloft
to urgent shouts and curses. Then silence
as eyes strain to see where two
copper coins fall equidistant.

Time for the stand-off—
Padna Hyland steadies the tosser,
two coins balanced on a sliver of wood.
Those small circles are hurled high,
tumbling briefly against the twilight sky.
Then necks crane, peering down again.
Head or hen? Or Irish harp?
(Across the border, a British crown.)

Voices soften in the darkness,
even oaths are muffled by half-light,
as a thin rain starts to fall
and the little stream whispers by.
Oh, the melancholy of Midland days!
In the thistled meadow beyond
the becalmed wreck of the Protestant church
a donkey raises its rusty bray.

The Deer Trap

There was a cave I visited, beside Barney Horisk's bog bank, a small wet cavern with a lattice of branches plaited over. It was near a stream, the insistent Garvaghey River, rattling over its pebbles. I would climb slowly down and ease myself into this secret space to sit there for hours in the semi-darkness, with shorts, and bare earth-caked feet. Crouched, legs drawn up, arms folded like fins across my narrow ribs, no sound but my own breathing; nothing to see but glints of sky through the plaited branches and the silver scrawls of snails down the turf walls.

What was I waiting for? The surprise of a head peering in, a head wearing antlers, the crash of a companion suddenly joining me as it collapses, shuddering, to its knees? We had come on it when we were digging turf, and felt it was different, something connected with faraway times. Men had driven down from the Ministry carrying instruments and maps and they had declared it was a deer trap, a deer pit; perhaps from the days when the Fianna had hunted their quarry through the great forests?

I hear the cold metal horns, I hear the hoarse cry of the hunting pack, the halloo of men on horses. For I am the hind crouched in darkness, breath rasping, hoping they will never find me, hoping to be found. A small rain begins to trickle down my back...

West Cork Annunciation

The Angel of the Lord declared unto Mary,
and she conceived of the Holy Ghost...

An austere kitchen, darker than the fields.
The Angelus sounds through the room.
Silently responding to its measured boom
Mary Kate interrupts our rambling talk
to bless herself, while Jackie doffs the big cap.

People of the past, grown tortoise-slow,
their world will have gone before they do.
Once hens flurried around the scullery door,
once the dog curled before the fire.
Now we sit, mesmerized, solemn,
drawn into the glow of the television.

An opulence of images invades the farmhouse,
girlish ikons from medieval France;
Sienese gravity: Raphael's rosy ecstasy.
What harm in this young Jewish bride,
pivot of their peasant world, her peasant child?
Would all our passions were as mild!

A turtle withdrawing into its shell,
Jackie puts back the cap; Mary Kate sighs,
thinking of something she can do for others,
tea to wet, or a whiskey glass to proffer;
she creaks across the room like a sailing ship.
And the Word was made flesh, and dwelt amongst us.

Prodigal Son

MacKillion, my first master of language,
calling, cursing the cattle at twilight
across the enfolding fields,
was a ritual, regular as a blessing,
challenging the silver peal of the Angelus

sounding through my aunts' Catholic kitchen
all the way from Athlone's *Radio Éireann*.
Big John loosed a stream of abuse:
'Big-arsed Polly, / I'll split your belly,'
as he beat them from the corners of the field,

battering their flanks with his big stick,
swaying *elders* swollen with milk.
'Big-diddied devil, / you're a right haveril.'
Their response, as hooves clattered on
the concrete yard, a splatter of dung.

Ganch, gulderer, gulpin, it rang,
a language hard, Northern, profane,
but with its own driving rhythm.
I wondered from what source it sprang,
and was my orphaned lot the same?

Carnaptious, cuttie and *caddie,*
I relished this new vocabulary,
scurrying home in my 'knickerbockers'
from 'the next block', to tell my *weemen*
I'd *bin kepping* the cows from the corn.

*

Long ago he had been taken in
by our neighbours, staunch Presbyterian,
To give a Catholic bye-child a home,
a tacit custom of that place and time,
rarely held to question, though

once old Mrs Clarke rebuked me when,
agent of my pious aunts, I accused them
of keeping him away from Mass:
'I would never come between
any man and his religion.'

                *

Loneliest of all, Big John
on the haggard wall at dusk, crooning
to himself *Drimindrew*, 'the tune
the old cow died of,' he said:
that harsh lament echoed in my head

against the picture of him all alone
beneath a sky grown brighter than
the twilight-grey whitewashed wall.
But why did he sing that solitary song
in the gloaming amidst the corn?

Years later I learnt it was a rune,
an *aisling*. An old Jacobite song,
An Droimeann Dubh, The Black
Cow, wandering forlorn through
the dew-wet fields of Ireland. But

innocence can undo anything.
As old age broke him slowly down

my aunts bribed and baited him
with a horn rosary, from this child's hand,
to rope his soul to its Papish home.

Too late I realized the damage done
as Big John marched past our window
to kneel, cramped as a draught horse,
in the chill Confession Box;
a chastened Prodigal Son.

A Fertile Balance

1.

The ring of pure light
on the table, bread and wine,
under the roof of baked tiles,
rooms cool as a pantry.
Stiff dried flowers and herbs
spice the oak beam's
fertile balance: an interior garden.

2.

Leaving, returning,
a round of ritual visits:
a tree creaks its slow greeting,
a windlass well, long deserted,
thickets of odorous lavender,
perfumed stone, a spade laid
in drills of aubergine, dense
and dark as hand grenades.

3.

A half century ago, the poet
hides in the brush, rifle
butt cradled against shoulder,
as the German convoy grinds near:
before he orders 'Fire!'
a brief scent of wild thyme.

4.

A warm day, the ochre earth
leaps before us: the khaki back,
bulging eye, of the cricket,
lofting away like a tiny helicopter
at an angle on its spindle legs.
The shrewd-eyed lizard sprawls,
then darts along a corbelled wall
in a continuous thrum of flies.

5.

Now the tall poet greets us
under his lintel, speaking
of rare flowers, scarce birds,
pollution in the rivers great
and small, the muscled Seine,
his homely Sorgue, the sun
on those waters darkening
as the trout turns belly up.

6.

'In the land of the day before,
the thunder rang pure in the streams,
the vine fostered the bee,
the shoulder lifted the burden.'
Now rocket ranges in the Vaucluse
the stink of Rhone Poulenc.
'Voters, students of your townland,
of its beasts and flowers, do not
falter in your duty. This is a call
to order, to halt the march of death.'

7.

Starless night over the Luberon,
the drone of a friendly plane,
a blossoming of parachutes;
the watchdog lopes between
them, nuzzling their freight
of guns and grenades, but
making no sound, neither bark
nor whimper, before dropping
to sleep on the crumpled silk.

8.

'I try not to go to Paris now,
source and centre of all this filth.'
Petrarch, fleeing southwards;
To redeem myself from that
pit of iniquity called Avignon
I fled to where a slate-blue

and white fountain pours,
while birds circle the cliff,
and drank till I felt restored.
Now when I make love
it is for the last time.

A Holy Show

for Kathleen Raine

Maybe John Scotus was the first to find out how
to lift that non-existent freight of Western thought,
a simple echo
of what the creators of the stone circles felt
lofting those tall shapes in the moonlight
the curve of planet earth
on which they briefly dwelt

with all those bright whirling worlds without.
No Platonic cave but a sparkling inside & out,
the air so champagne clear
they could have reached to grasp a star
through the crystalline atmosphere, like a candle
or the rush-light burning in their
neighbour's hut next door.

So the soul will sail when its time has come
to quit its earthly sheath and wander around & in
as the thrice blessed Hermes
says, and all the sages know,
the same above as here below,
the galaxy a holy show.

Demolition Ireland

for Sibyl

Observe the giant machines trundle over
this craggy land, crushing old contours,
trampling down the nearly naked earth.
Dragon rocks dragged into the open,
dislodged from their primaeval dream.
River banks, so slowly, lushly formed,
haunt of the otter and waterhen,
bulldozed into a stern, straight line;
dark trout pools dredged clean
so that doomed cattle may drink any time.
Once mysteries coiled in the tangled clefts
of weed and whin, land left to itself...
But see, the rushes rise again, by stealth,
tireless warriors, on the earth's behalf.

Last of the House*

The mountains drowse
around us, each evening.
We almost understand them,

their gorse-tough slopes
where more has happened
than we can grasp.

In this valley no one
lifts a fiddle and no
one speaks Irish.

Though once we heard
Mount Gabriel singing
for an O'Driscoll dying:

the last of his house.
Even the sheep, still
as boulders on the slopes,

lifted their heads
to attend this numinous sound.
Interweaving voices, male

and female, echoing
from the mountain side;
a spectral opera

of loving sorrow;
fierce calamity,
stubborn continuity.

* Based on the Irish phrase An Fear Deiranach den tSloinne: The Last of the Clan.

Family Rosary

1.

The rasp and scrape of wood on stone.
We kneel in a circle of chairs.
Aunt Brigid's has a broken frame,
Aunt Freda steadies a rocker's crescent.
I scuff the arm of a threadbare armchair.

*

As the steady drone deepens,
Hail Mary dissolving into Holy Mary,
I bury my head in the musty cushions,
tease their tassels in boyish boredom

until Aunt Brigid leads the final prayers,
a voice raised against the night,
assuming response, numbering the dead
with claim on these frail living

who sigh in their separate reveries
of Sorrowful and Joyful mysteries
while the beads glide through fingers —
grain sliding from a sack.

*

And the walls fade and change,
the lights dwindle under the holy picture
with its soft pierced hands;
the fire is sucked up the chimney,
the traffic swallows the road.

2. THE TRIMMINGS

Garrulous Berryman, break the Mississippi ice
like a seal, with a fresh sonnet for us;
strict Marianne, sport your black cartwheel
of a hat again, at Ebbet's Field:

Señor Graves, lead the company gladly,
in Cork or Mallorca, with an Irish *come-all-ye*,
MacDiarmid, with tough terrier intensity,
share a rare Highland Malt with us,

while Austin, lover of Erato, lifts
a thin glass, a Winter's Tale, and
David Jones and his crony, René,
grow merry upon Rose's Lime Juice Cordial.

Now that my admired dead begin
to overtake the living, I might muster
a new litany of ghostly recruits
so that all the good and gifted dead
may strengthen the hands of the living:
to work as well, in death's shade,
and not lose heart, or faith.

Wreaths

I. A Good Bye

René Hague, you endured your hospital bed
with thin rolled cigarettes, and mild soldier's curses,
until they informed you that your wife was dead
and your own disease terminal. Then you turned
your lean face to the wall, after a formal farewell:

you gave me back the books you had borrowed,
George Herbert's The Temple, and Dante's Paradiso,
then, lifting my hand to your sere lips,
sighed Goodbye. The memory of such grace
is a rare liqueur from which memory sips.

2. Civil War Veteran

i.m. C S (Todd) Andrews

At the cigar and brandy stage
an old civil war veteran recalls
someone he killed — a half secret —
or someone he missed — a half regret.

Somehow it now amounts to the same thing.
'Sure, he'd be dead, or —' (half-laughing,
blinking age-cowled saurian eyes)
'— half-dying now, like myself.'

Last Court

Poetry, 'tis a court of judgement upon the soul.
— Henrik Ibsen

1. Non Piangere

From your last chair,
two months before that glutton, cancer,
devoured you, lawyer brother,
you gave me a final wigging, read the riot act,
as if I were some juvenile delinquent
hauled before the magistrate.

This sun-warm conservatory,
latest addition to your ultra-modern bungalow
overlooking Brown-Lecky's estate
(now manicured golf course), recalls the deck
of that Cunard liner, the Cameronia,
which, ages ago, shipped us boys to Fintona.

Home again, in mid-Tyrone,
you built your now fading life,
fathering a tribe within a tribe,
only to chide me now, for my 'great mistake,
repeated, *twice*', of choosing a wife
from the wider world outside.

'They don't understand. You need somebody
who thinks like you, shares your beliefs.'
Mildly, I place a picture of your two nieces
(my Cork, French, Jewish,
Church of Ireland children)
upon your knee, for loving avuncular scrutiny.

But you sigh it away
and, having pronounced your last verdict,
stalk off to rest, dying, but striding with dignity,
without a whimper of self-pity,
through your assembled family,
your last gift, this fragile bravery.

2.

To leave me forever with your disapproval,
yet rueful love, and a contradictory testimony,
'Strangely, I have never felt so happy, as now,
giving up, letting go, floating free.'
You look down, pensively, at your glass
of burnished Black Bush whiskey.

'And, no, I no longer pray,
although I talk to God sometimes in my head.
And our parents. Why did you hurt our mother's pride

with your mournful auld poem, *The Dead Kingdom*?
Only a child, you couldn't understand their decision:
besides, you got the details wrong!'

'So you believe we'll see them again?
Bone-light, transfigured, Molly and Jim,
angels dancing upon a pin, and then
I can take it up with them again?'
'No,' you say stubbornly, 'never again,'
shaking your once-red Ulster head.

And plucking your pallid, freckled arm,
'I don't believe,' you proclaim,
'in the body's resurrection.
See how the flesh wastes parchment-thin?'
Yet, resigned as the Dying Gaul,
stoic as an ancient Roman.

3. UN GRIDO LACERANTE

Dear freckled brother, in an old photo,
you throw your arm around me
in a Brooklyn park, your impulse to hug
preserved there for posterity.
Let me reverse our roles, carefully as I can,
to encircle you, this time, with *my* arm.

In far off Florence, I learnt of your death;
Evelyn calling from a rain-swept West Cork.
'It was a merciful release,' that cliché — yet true.
'But how can I trek all that way North?
My sister's children are here, as well as our own.
It's a long hard slog up to County Tyrone.'

Phone to my ear, gazing out at the Arno,
I hear, behind her, the laughter of children,
those nieces whose picture you dismissed.
'Cherish the living, while honouring the dead,
I'll stand over that, pray they'll comprehend.
The church bells of Florence will bless him instead.'

As many mourners assemble at your funeral
in our chill and distant Northern chapel,
since you loved paintings I patrol
the Pitti, the Uffizi, turning from
a foam-borne Botticelli nymph, or
grave Madonna, to weep above Dante's city:

sharp-tempered, once you smashed me to the floor
in our mother's kitchen, and standing over
me, like some American boxer, 'Rise
and fight like a man'—and I only sixteen!
Aproned Molly hovering, a hapless referee;
you stalk away, to return with a brusque apology.

Sharp-tempered but kindly, you drove
your poet brother home from Dublin,
emptying my squalid flat without reproach.
Later, wives and lives came between us,
differing codes of conduct and belief.
Yet I still glimpse your ginger hair and freckle face.

Long before the cancer struck I saw that face
grown ashen, fissured as chalk, suddenly old
as though some secret source had parched,
and sought to tell you, *Relax again*,
as when you roamed Bundoran with the Fintona gang.
But tact forbade. Or cowardice?

Now, hear my plea. Sweet-souled Santayana
might have agreed with you, brother, about exogamy,
but against your patriarchal views,
I assert the right of love to choose,
from whatever race, or place. And of verse
to allay, to heal, our tribal curse, that narrowness.

First Landscape, First Death

So deep this landscape lies
in me; I try to leave it behind,
but again and again it returns,
burning with its secret light.

            Russet bog
loses itself in a blue distance,
a curlew laments overhead,
and again I become that displaced
child, wandering these lanes, break-
ing a stick from these hedges,
to lash the crowns off thistles,
pressing purple foxglove fingers
together to yield a brief burst
of sound, exploring the mystery
of an old limekiln where a heifer
licks her calf.

            My father
wanted to be buried here
and before Aunt Mary died
she asked her son to drive her
around these same rough hills

(but with their secret lushness),
after the hard care of marriage
and children, to re-find the girl
who once wandered there.

*

Big Allie Owens crunched down
the lane in her high-buttoned boots
to collect her pension and provisions.
When she grew too old I had
to haul the basket to her. Thick
crusted shop bread, planks of ribboned
bacon, fed that mare's stomach:
oven and skillet suspended
on black hooks over a turf fire.

Abandoned by her doctor,
the priest came to reconcile her,
to measure her for the long fight
towards death. I sat by her bedside
after school watching the dark grow
against the pines, where the crows
sank to rest, and heard her groan
against her fate. Large-limbed
as a cart horse, she died hard.

But first, slowly, she gave away
all she had to her neighbours.
I got a shoal of bright half-crowns,
but to Kitty Horisk, with her children,
'There's a wheen of sovereigns
under the mattress, all for you.'
For everyone, something. And still
they came, competing in friendliness,

carrying sweet water from the well,
new wheaten bread, until the end.

*

So, for myself, I would seek
no other final home, than
this remote country hiding place,
which gave me gentle nourishment
when I was most in need of it;
and still gives solace. In dream
I leap across stone through stream,
stride from road to lane. And even
moving light-footed between
cities where I am known
I am stopped suddenly by
the sight of some distant hill
or curving twilight river, to see
on a ghostly mound, my abiding
symbol, a weathered standing stone.

Slievemore

1.

When this landscape has been
absorbed into the mind
taken up into the dream

a single image may flake
away, flint or obsidian,
to reveal a whole civilization.

2.

Called up
by thunder clap
by draughts of rain

the bronze doors
of the evening sky open
and I shiver to discern

massively
glinting in the watery sun:
Slievemore's guardian forms.

3.

Jagged head
of warrior, bird
of prey, surveying space

side by side
they squat, the stern
deities of this place,

giant arms
slant to the calm
of lap, kneebone;

blunt fingers
splay to caress
a rain-hollowed stone

towards which
the landscape of five parishes
tends, band after band

of final,
peewit haunted,
cropless bogland.

from

SPEECH LESSONS

(2011)

Speech Lesson

for Michael Longley

1.

The chant of those carriage wheels
as we chug towards Belfast;
clickety-click, lickety-split,
When will I learn again to speak?

A straggle of villages before Dungannon:
Beragh, Carrickmore, Sixmilecross
(forlorn stations, later bypassed)
or *Will I never, ever speak again?*

2. THE FLOWER

After hilly Dungannon, holy Donaghmore.
A cluster of convent girls clambers
aboard the train, sweep and swirl
past the place of the tongue-tied boy
who huddles his head in his book
(which suddenly sheds all importance)
while they pile into the next compartment.
A chatter-and-clatter like starlings
as they settle. But one, bolder,
tiptoes along the swaying corridor
to risk a look where he sits, blushing.
Then another. A flurry of giggles.
Though as the troop leaves, prodding one another,
the bold one turns to throw him a flower.

3.

Under the leather seats the creak
of iron wheels as we steam towards Belfast:
When will I learn again to speak?
The Calvin Mills at Portadown,
Balmoral Showgrounds, and tethered
above the wartime city, a silvery barrage balloon.
(Belfast's knell had not yet rung.)

4.

Near the bulky City Hall, 20 Wellington.
An ardent young Englishwoman,
speaking of War and Poetry,
places a hand on his tummy-tum-tum,
(the first stranger to have so done).
'Young man, learn to speak from your diaphragm:
Many merry men marched many times.
And you should read Drummond Allison.
He was stationed here in Northern Ireland.'
She presses down, again and again:
'Consider our King: he broadcasts, stammering.
So let the wind whistle through your lungs.
And read poetry aloud, it can be such fun!
From how far away did you say you've come?'

5.

Clickety-click, clickety-clack as
the Derry evening train ferries him back
all the way to County Tyrone and

Beragh station, a lantern swaying
along the platform. The parting whistle.
Then the long pull on his bicycle
through the hay-scented countryside
to the turf-heavy hearth at home,
the Rosary and a mug of Ovaltine
in the Sacred Heart–flushed kitchen.
Candle in hand he climbs to his room.
A scurry of giggles, the shock of that flower.
Many weary men marched many times:
Shall I begin to speak again?

I can still smell her perfume.

Baldung's Vision

I saw a tiny Christ
caper on the cross

silent as a salamander
writhing in fire

or a soldier triumphant
when the battle's lost;

wine bursts from
his body's grapeskin:

'The suffering you see
is our daily mystery,

so follow my body
as it sings mutely

(a lantern, a ladder,
a window, a pathway)

of pain calcined away
in a dance of ecstasy.'

Silences

for Elizabeth

1.

Poetry is a weapon and should be used,
though not in the crudity of violence.
It is a prayer before an unknown altar,
a spell to bless the silence.

2.

There is a music beyond all this,
beyond all forms of grievance,
where anger lays its muzzle down
into the lap of silence.

3.

Or some butterfly script,
fathomed only by the other,
as supple fingers draw
a silent message from the tangible.

Vendange

for Pierre Joannon

Mists and mellow fruitfulness —
as we cycle through the dawn
along the great river Marne,
a pal from still-dormant Derry
and myself, passing out each other,
sturdy Raleigh against low-slung Racer,

to toil all day amid the vines
shearing the grapes with the claws,
the jaws of the iron secateurs,
then hoisting our cloudy burden
of green-gold champagne grapes
in their great woven baskets.

Close bosom-friend of the maturing sun —
the harvest heat beat down
bold and brazen as a gong,
but we were wild and young,
Keats and Rimbaud in my rucksack,
On n'est pas sérieux, quand on a dix-sept ans.

*

Our reward, to dance and sing in
the village square each evening
to the yearning cadence of an accordion,
our arms that all day curved round
rush baskets curve now round waists;
though as midnight strikes the girls
melt away, laughing faintly, and
we ride back to our spartan hostel.

Sundays we tramped the countryside,
two lanky Irish lads, slowly growing aware
of what desolation had been wrought there,
the earth trenched with wounds:
for beyond the local *Monuments aux Morts*
sprawled Allied and German cemeteries
stored with vintage blood, strange wineries.
La terre est nubile et débordé de sang.

While barred clouds bloom the soft-dying day —
the punctual magic of the train,
each evening the long, lit Rheims Express
passing through on her way to Paris.
Listening to the carriages' swaying clatter
I did not yet know they were ferrying
my own future towards and away from me.
Le Soleil, le foyer de tendresse et de vie.

Keats and Rimbaud jostling in my rucksack,
On est trop sérieux, quand on a dix-huit ans!

In My Grandfather's Mansion

1.

In my grandfather's library
there were many volumes,

Bibles massive as flagstones,
heavy print my eye could trawl along:

the thunder of the Old Testament.

I climbed the Mount with Moses,
stood in the presence of the Lord,
or listened as he spake from a cloud.

For, lo, I had suffered the long exodus
from Brooklyn and New York
where they worshipped the Golden Calf

which now staggers, newly born,
rasped clean by its mother's tongue,
on the cobblestones of our farmyard.

2.

I chanted the *Proverbs* and *Psalms*
and later bathed in the *Song of Songs*:

Thy love is headier than wine,
honey and milk lie under thy tongue,
thy lips ... drip as the honeycomb.

To what dark-eyed maiden
might I yet sing such a song?

Lily of the valley, rose of Sharon...

3.

Matthew, Mark, Luke and John
blessed the bed I lay upon.

My grandfather's bed in my grandfather's room;
but I loved the *Revelations* of yet another John,

he of Patmos: *a woman clothed with the sun,*
a two-horned lamb who spoke like a dragon —

locusts, with breastplates of iron;
the heads of the horses as heads of lions.

The *Apocalypse,* God's Horror Comic!
Like the scary film, with Boris Karloff,

I had seen on my last day in Brooklyn
and can remember as the rats scamper

above the damp-blotched wallpaper
in the shadowy rafters over my head.

The beams of our house are cedar,
and our rafters of fir...

James Whale's *House of the Dead*
seen by a small boy, now transplanted.

4.

Christmas stars stud the sky
as in my grandfather's bed I lie.

'*What are you doing in my bedroom,*
plundering my library, perusing my will?
Where the devil did you come from?'

'John begat James who begat John.
Why did you sire so many children,
you old goat, with luxuriant beard

and sideburns? I am second generation
fruit of your loins, who has come from afar
to dwell with your two maiden daughters,
your eldest, Brigid, your youngest, Winifred,
in that rural empire you founded.'

'Like Ruth amid the alien corn!'

'Except I was born in Depression Brooklyn,
a raw raucous place you have never seen,
with clanging trolleys and lurid neon.'

'So you were born in America
where they had that terrible Civil War:
Meagher of the Sword, at Fredericksburg,
where over a thousand Irish died,
sporting "their sprigs of green".

'Look at those photographs of slaughtered
soldiers, arranged by Mathew Brady,
next to Whitman, in my library.'

'With Butler's Lives of the Saints
and Vasari's Lives of the Artists:
at least you were catholic in your tastes!'

'And in my thoughts: Cardinals Wiseman
and Manning, conducting their lofty debates
around the Immaculate Conception,
ponderous and Victorian to you, perhaps.
Though Catholic I served the Queen
as postmaster and lay magistrate:
a bleak land, after the Famine.
No need to read the Riot Act

(white gloves often on the bench),
a small cog in the Imperial machine:
the greatest Empire ever seen.'

'And, lo, led your people out of Egypt,
downhill, that is, from Altamuskin,
and Altcloghfin, to this Broad Road
that sweeps from Derry to Belfast.'
(Years later, in troubled dreams,
I hear ghostly carriages rumble past.)

5.

'My grandfather's clock was too tall for the shelf
so he spent forty years in the bed,
going tick-tock, tick-tock,
until he stopped short,
never to go again
in Garvaghey graveyard.'

Many years without slumbering
(Tick-tock, tick-tock),
many children engendering...
I saw his grave dug open
to admit another daughter,
sired in that same iron bed
I now occupy, listening
to the rodents rustling overhead.

His thigh bone seemed enormous,
large as the *jawbone of an ass,*
but I was only an altar boy
clothed in mystic surplice and soutane

(over New World knickerbockers)
to serve her Funeral Mass, before
the fresh clods struck the coffin,
brass handles, polished wood.
For dust thou art,
and unto dust shalt thou return...

6.

'That ditty should have stuck in your throat!
Why must you strike such a vulgar note?
Without me you would not even exist,
so a little courtesy would not go amiss!'

'Listen, you auld fecker, you may be my grandfather
but the round world has rolled on since then.'

'And completely lost its manners?'

'You had Cardinals: Manning, Wiseman, Newman,
ruminating over the Immaculate Contraption.
My heroes were Tiger Flowers, and Slapsy Maxy Rosenbloom,
and then the Brown Bomber, and Billy Conn;
livelier than your solemn, red-hatted procession.
Did you never play stoop-ball, put nickels under trolley or tram?'

'Brash as an American, you don't sound
like my grandson, or even an Ulsterman!
Do you know Newman's definition of a Gentleman?
"A Gentleman is one who never inflicts pain"—
Study that for a while, then speak to me again.
Besides, larger families were common then.'

'But what would your poor wife have to say?'

7.

But who was my grandmother?
Silence. Or almost.
Her name I learnt was Quinn
(pronounced, locally, *Queen*),
the robust one of several sisters
afflicted with consumption,
wasting away slowly, slowly
in the house across from our own.

(The Lynches and I played
in its ruins, wrestling in our dungarees
amidst swollen grainsacks as
bats looped through broken windows;
unaware of where we were, walls
blighted by illness, now
shrunken to a storehouse
for horses, cattle, hay.)

And I have only one photograph
of a tightly corseted woman.
She unlaced them ritually
for my grandfather's embrace
in this same iron bed,
night after patriarchal night,
until she died, in childbirth.

A grandparent myself,
I say a word for her now,
a silent, solemn figure
lost in the shadows
of a doomed place:
before she crosses the road,

through the portals of our house,
into male energy and merriment.

In my grandmother's time one woman
was Queen of the known world
(another, Virgin Queen of the unknown),
so shall I name her our Lost Queen,
Our Lady of Shadows, Our Lady of 'Shall Not',
a patient figure at her spinning wheel
without whom I would not have been?

8.

'Out of the darkness I dare to speak.
I am not the silent Queen
of Garvaghey and Altcloghfin,
I am not a plaster saint,
I am not a figurine.

'If my John can speak
across a century's silence,
why should I stay mute:
I was a flesh-and-blood woman,
the strongest of my house,
so do not distil me into dream!

'But how the men were spoilt,
grouped in the parlour,
scarcely bothering to lift their plates
to help us when we served,
dunting like sucking calves
as we ladled out their portions,
then back to the talk and drink again.'

(And, abashed, I recall
a rare flash of anger from Aunt Brigid:
'All the men together, playing cards
and drinking whiskey, while
we hungry children cried.')

9.

Whitman saw Ireland 'an ancient sorrowful mother,
once a queen, now lean and tatter'd...'
'Will you have a titter of wit, man,

or I'll push you before my besom.
There were mouths agape, bottoms to clean,
cows to milk, and churns to turn,

a hearth-crook heavy with pots and pans,
farls of soda and wheaten bread.
I was far smarter than most men,

though I left all the gabble to them.
And you seem to forget I loved my John,
he was a fine figure of a man,

handsome as Victoria's German one:
Did you know that every night in Windsor
Albert's clothes were laid out on the bed,

and she slept with his picture over her head?
She presided over her unfurling world:
India, Africa, the Crimea and Khartoum,

as I presided over mine, Garvaghey, Altcloghfin,
pressing the treadles of my sewing machine.
So wasn't I happy to have my John

and that lively bunch of children?
And wasn't he the great reader,
though only a class of hedge schoolmaster?

(That scringe of chalk on slate.)
He was so pleased when Cousin Joseph
became a Cardinal, with his book on Prophet John.

And who are you, anyway, you whippersnapper,
sharing our family secrets with the world:
so I say again, have a titter of wit, man!'

Many Mansions

In my grandfather's house there were many mansions.

In the dim back shelves of the shop
lay serried rows of dicky bows.
Where were the gentlemen who wore them?
Arrayed in Garvaghey graveyard in rows...

I hid in one of the empty tea chests
inhaling the aroma of India or China
where a great war was waging as
I crinkled the strips of tin foil.

A squat barrel of molasses
stood in the cellar, exuding a thick sweetness
like the dull nectar of wasps,
while from their dank corner
the sickly white tendrils of
the seed potatoes strained
towards the almost lunar light
of the spider-gauzed window.

But most ghostly, the line of mannequins
along the long shed. Those women
who had once sported antique hats, lace blouses,
long skirts, even ball gowns,
now endured my embrace of their wire limbs,
a small boy sticking his fingers into their metal midriffs
as I ferried them from place to place.

I tried to dance with them
but the metal scraped and tangled
in our slow stiff waltz,
so I toppled them over one by one
until they lay still as the dicky bows on their shelf.

Patience and Time

Winifred Montague (1900–1983)

Patience and time
will bring the snail
to Jerusalem...
my Aunt Winifred's favourite saying
as she sits playing Patience

after she had spent hours
mucking out the byre,
wearing man's boots or wellies,
then straddling the runnel
to wash it down.

Or wheeling the barrow
heavy with dung to
the mound of the dunghill:
hardly the occupation

for a bright convent girl
summoned all the way
from college quad to farmyard
when Ireland divides
and her brothers slide into bankruptcy.

Or balancing on a stool,
leaning against the warm
flank of a feeding heifer,
squeezing and squirting
the swollen teats until
they fill the frothing pail.

Patience and time
bring the snail to Jerusalem:
I see the tiny pilgrim
on his gleaming liquid course;
his periscopic horns,
his silver slide forward.

Or whirling the churn,
the slosh of the cream,
until a yellow gleam
lights the small window:
I glimpse the Golden Dome
of his tireless dream.

In the winter evenings
Patience, or Solitaire,
by the tilley lamp.
Card falls on card
upon the baize table:
no matter how hard
there is no complaint,
no thunder against fate.

As numbers mount
from Ace to Ten,
according to suit,
and a red row climbs
beside the black:
Spades against Diamonds,
Clubs against Hearts,
Queens fall on Jacks,
Kings fall on Queens

and the snail halts.

from

SECOND CHILDHOOD

(2017)

Summer Snow

I dreamt a dream of madness
beside a sunstruck sea:
the snow lay thick in August,
chill flakes cloaking me.

To you alone could I tell it
for you alone could know
how by the sea in August
the sky was full of snow.

(1948)

The Afterlife of Dogs

I tried to come between
my dog and his dying
in a dark corner of our barn,

cajoling him
to wag his tail
(as he had always done)

but he wanted none of it,
though he licked my hand.

Next morning he was dead.
We buried him in a corner
of our garden. I did not know

then that dying is an art
which dogs have mastered:
their frail show of love

a final dignity.
Over the years several
would follow him,

even old Flo, drowsing
in front of the house, lumbered
over by the Post-Office van.

Seven dogs beneath the rhubarb,
beside our lorry-laden road.

Star Song

for Joseph Voelker

The stars still sing,
even if, clamorous mortals,
we cannot hear them
chorusing their silver music,
silent nocturnes.

A new astronomy is needed —
to marry the scientific
and mythical,
the musical and magical,
the gleaming mathematical.

As a child I lay,
trying to hear them,
like the astronomer princes
of the Old World:
keeping a vigil,
attending a miracle.

Ferret

Its button snout flickers
from its straw-lined litter,
querying, questing:
the unlikely snake-
dance of a rodent.

Sore red eyes,
a small drunk
on his urgent mission:
sniffing the wind
for a curer of blood.

It undulates up
Austin's freckled arm
with sleek affection:
its servant function
to insinuate corners

no terrier could negotiate,
slithering smugly down
to darkness, disappearance,
needle-teeth unsheathed.
The silence chills

to the cry of a rabbit,
soft throat gripped,
then slowly hauled
in tremulous throes
into sudden daylight.

*

Soon the glove resumes
its owner's arm, a slack-
necked rabbit dangling
from the other hand, still
warm, still twitching.

Alight

When a girl I adored at Glencull School
appeared as an angel in the Christmas play
my heart 'soared and fluttered' *et cetera*,

while she tiptoed, dipped and sang
to light the tapering candles:
as each wick unfurled I lit up inside.

Her hair was long and princess-yellow
(or so I thought) with a silver circlet
on her brow: *a ghost-light now.*

When she brushed past me in the corridor,
then paused to turn and kiss me
all in one happy swooping stride,

and I felt the flare of her tinsel
wings as they briefly enfolded me,
I came alive, like a Christmas tree.

Scotia

in memory of Hugh MacDiarmid

We have come so far North,
farther than we have ever been
to where gales strip everything
and the names ring guttural
syllables of old Norse:
Thurso, Scrabster, Laxdale,
names that clang like a battleaxe.

Then farther West. There beauty
softens, a darkening estuary,
Farr or Borgie or Skerray where
waist-high in shallow waters
silent shadows cast at night
to lasso the lazily feeding trout
which gleam on our hotel plate.

Still farther, mountains gather,
blue peak lifting beyond blue peak,
Ben Loyal and then Ben Hope,
noble, distant as the Twelve Bens
or Brandon; single tracks on
endless moors, or threading along
the flanks of melancholy lochs.

Loch Loyal and Loch Naver
where Alpine flowers blossom,
the wilderness's blessing;
as MacDiarmid will proudly remark
in our last, rambling conversation,
'Strange, lovely things grow up there,
ecologically *vairy* inter-resting.'

By such roads, only sheep prosper,
bending to crop the long acre,
or whiten the heather, like bog cotton.
The name of this county, Sutherland,
synonym for burnings, clearances,
the black aura of Castle Dunrobin,
stone cottages broken, like Auburn.

We are not Thirties aesthetes, leaving
on impulse for 'Cape Wrath tonight'
but fellow Gaels who have come
as far as the Kyle of Tongue
to see a sister country, Scotland,
or what is left of it, before
Scotia, like Wallia, is plundered.

Along the new motorway
trucks and trailers strain, an invasion
grinding from England, the Grampians
pushed aside, in search of wealth;
the North Sea's blackening pulse,
the rigs towed from Moray Firth
to prop a fading imperial strength.

Beyond Tongue, still rises Ben Hope
and that star of mountains, Suilven,
which beckons to an intent fisherman:
MacCaig, with whom I share a patronym.
His unswerving eye and stylish line
pierce through flesh to the dying bone.
May Scotland always have such fishermen

nourishing a lonely dream of how
this desolate country might have been.

The rightful arrogance of MacDiarmid's
calling together of Clann Albann,
or the surging lamentations of MacLean,
the sound of his echoing Gaelic
a fierce pibroch crying on the wind.

Ritual of Grief

After Mary Kate died
her brother, Jacky, sat
in gathering darkness,
obeying by instinct
an injunction ancient
as their West Cork hills:

Shroud the mirrors
to eschew all vanity

Take off shoes
to show humility

Quench the lights
to attain solemnity

Leave off the radio
to foster silence

but for the clock high on the wall,
measuring time, strict and forlorn.

Children's Sorrows

Children's sorrows,
abrupt, overwhelming;
a raindrop trembling
on a butterfly's wing.

Cry

As I work quietly
by a large window
overlooking the sea
I hear a sudden cry,
intense and terrible.

Did someone strike a child
or lash a cringing dog?
I straighten and turn
to see workmen
surround a large

and green-leafed tree
which they are cutting down
with old-fashioned axes.
The green-and-white entrails,
the clash-and-shudder of branches,

summon a victim of some savagery.
But worse is the cry. Centuries of life
are poured into that sound. And after
they are done, the tree felled,
that cry goes on, absorbed by the sea

and thrown back.

Sonnet for Berryman

A note to celebrate our days together,
memories to warm that dank Dublin winter,
hot toddies in Beggars Bush as you distil
another run from your fermenting Dream Songs.
I was still young, aghast at genius,
concerned with your comfort, a practical worshipper.
Later you came looking for me in Paris.
Claude Esteban, beneath his cameo
of Baudelaire, found you on his doorstep;
white-bearded, demanding in stentorian tones
'Ou est le poète irlandais?' and
Claude soft-footed across the way:
'Il y a un Moise* américain que te demande!'
Behind him Henry Pussycat, grinning from ear to ear.

*Moise: Moses

Hopkins in Dublin

After reading Father Hopkins—
his Terrible Sonnets—
I listen to the Blues,
a bittersweet voice rising
over a vivid trumpet,
a shuddering saxophone;
salvos of sadness
replenishing the soul.

And imagine our delicate priest
hearkening to these bodily rhythms,
these moonshine harmonies,

perhaps stirred to dance
or at least to shuffle,
swaying his cassock
around his spartan bedroom.

*

Gerard, are you grieving
over Stephen's Green unleaving?
Things were hard for you in Dublin,
a shy John Bull among Fenians,
constantly ragged about politics;
uproar in the classrooms: 'the great,
very great, drudgery of examinations'.

But you spent your last Christmas
beside the 'burling Barrow brown'.
And I have climbed to your room
in 86 St Stephen's Green,
lofty and lonely but blessed
with a view of the Iveagh Gardens,
the plum-soft Dublin mountains.

Enniskerry, the Scalp,
the Powerscourt waterfall,
the white cone of the Sugarloaf
(where, aflush with your poetry,
I dallied with a girl): Why
did you never inscape *them*?

And in a summersunny Phoenix Park
you laughed when a cricketer cried,
as he struck a boundary,
Arrah, sweet meself. As now
we cherish your boundary-breaking gift.

The Leap

To find a wider
more impossible spot,
the ultimate leap
beyond Lynch's meadow —

rock-girdled,
a deep, dark, circling
turnhole that could
swirl over my head.

A task to which
I slowly nerve myself,
circling always nearer,
until late one night —

closing my eyes —
I take off and find
myself on the far
ledge, scrabbling.

Secret wellsprings
of strength, forgotten
disciplines of night,
those long, lovely

leaps in the dark
return now to steady
my mind, nourish
my courage as —

no longer young—
I take your hand
to face a different,
more frightening task:

defying convention
for love's sake,
leaving behind ground
tested and safe,

using a lesson learnt
long ago in Lynch's meadow,
circling the task
to vault the flow

and taking off again
into the uncertain dark,
hoping to land safely
on a far warm bank.

Index of First Lines